Touched
by the
Grace of God

Touched
by the
Grace of God

by

Heidi R. May, RDH

AuthorHouse™
1663 Liberty Drive
Bloomington, IN 47403
www.authorhouse.com
Phone: 1-800-839-8640

Published by AuthorHouse   02/18/2012

ISBN: 978-1-4490-2268-6 (sc)
ISBN: 978-1-4685-2885-5 (e)

Library of Congress Control Number: 2011962551

Cover and layout designed by Lana May.

This
book
is
dedicated
to
all of God's children. I pray that they will be
blessed
by
His
infinite
love,
mercy,
and
grace
throughout
their
lives.

· ❀ ·

Preface

TWO EVENTS POWERFULLY AFFECTED my spiritual life over the past twelve years: reading Janice T. Connell's book, *The Visions of the Children* and experiencing miracles at Angel Kisses gift shop in St. Charles, Illinois. The first time I read Janice's book, I heard the Blessed Mother Mary call my name and I could smell the fragrance of Christ while rereading her book. I gradually began to make changes in my life. I received reconciliation, forgave others, and prayed more often. I also began fasting on bread and water on Wednesdays and Fridays. I fasted this way for about seven years. Over several years of visiting Angel Kisses gift shop I experienced a variety of wonderful blessings.

My religion has changed over the years. I have always been a Christian. I was raised as a Methodist, became a Lutheran for a few years when my mother married a Lutheran, and began attending the Catholic Church when I married a Catholic. During this time I was not a perfect Christian but now know that I am forgiven. God does not have a list of sins that He does **not** forgive. He forgives instantly and permanently no matter what we have done.

I have been a dental hygienist for more than thirty years. During this time I have shared and heard interesting stories at work. Many of my patients and friends repeatedly encouraged me to record and document my stories for a book. I began to make notations about my special experiences on calendars and summarize those events at the end of each year. This seemed to be a reasonable idea, but I was concerned about my writing ability. I considered the possibility and prayed about it for months before I decided to give it a try. Since all of the stories were true, I believed that I would merely need to organize them. Now, years after I started the book, I can say it was more difficult than I envisioned.

Hearing that you have cancer is a wake-up call to living. This news causes you to seriously consider your own mortality and contemplate any unfinished endeavors in your life. Writing this book was one of the projects I felt I needed to attempt during the remainder of my life. About one year after my breast cancer surgery, I decided to begin the book.

I began to realize that most of my stories would be relatively brief. I hoped I would be able to encourage others to share their stories, and then I would have enough stories for an entire book.

I didn't want anyone to feel I was trying to make a profit from his or her story; that is why I decided to donate my royalties to a charity. I had to decide which charity should receive the money. One day I tried remembering one of my five favorite charities. My mind was completely blank. Then I tried to remember one of fifteen other charities to which I had occasionally supported. I couldn't believe that I could not remember one of twenty charities I had donated money to over the past twenty-five years. Then the words "St. Jude's Hospital" scrolled across my blank mind, just like the stock market quotes scroll by on a ticker tape. (St. Jude Children's Research Hospital wasn't even one of the twenty charities.) God text-messaged my mind! I said, "I'll do it."

When I began writing I felt compelled to call the book "By the Grace of God," but after a couple of years I felt that the title lacked something. I believed that I needed to add to the title, but somehow I never found the correct words.

About two years later, during a phone conversation with one of the book's contributors, God helped me realize the precise title. The woman I was speaking with asked me what the title of the book was. I knew that sometime earlier I had told her, but she forgot. I explained that I was in the process of changing it, but for the time being I was still calling the book "By the Grace of God." She said, "Heidi, this did not come from me, but while you were telling me the name of your book the word 'Touched' was placed in my mind. You are supposed to call your book *Touched by the Grace of God*." I immediately said, "I love it!"

After hearing some of my stories, several people have asked me, "How come all the good stuff happens to you?" The Bible tells us in Ephesians 4:7, "But to each one of us grace was given according to the measure of Christ's gift." This means that we are all included in God's grace, and He will decide the degree of grace we will receive.

As you read these stories, I hope you will feel uplifted, renewed in faith, and closer to God; and that you pay close attention to small details around you. All of these stories are true and were provided by the grace of God. Some names have been changed in a few of the stories. All of the story contributors felt touched by the grace of God, even if it was just a subtle experience. My personal stories are in section one and are mostly in chronological order. The remaining stories are from my patients, friends, friends of friends or their relatives, and other special individuals. I attempted to convey the stories exactly as they were told to me.

You may view photographs and supporting documents at:
www.touchedbythegraceofGod.com
www.facebook.com (Enter *Touched by the Grace of God* in the search window.)

· ❖ ·

Acknowledgments

I HAVE A MULTITUDE of people to thank. May God abundantly bless all of the contributors and editors. There are so many people who lovingly and joyfully contributed their stories, taking time to share their experiences, so that others could read about them and be filled with faith, inspiration, and hope.

My husband is the only one who truly realized how much time I spent creating this book—more than seven years. I thank him for his patience and ask God to bless him.

I would like to thank my dear friend Agnes Hielsher for her contributions. Agnes encouraged my efforts throughout the years.

I especially need to thank Maryann Penczak. Maryann was just as enthusiastic about this project as I was, and God knew I needed her expertise to complete this project. This book was a labor of love for both of us. I knew we could overcome any obstacles we might encounter, when I smelled the fragrance of Christ near us as we looked over the first group of stories.

I could not, in a thousand years, adequately thank Michelle Peiser, Diane Olson,

Jeremy Gertzfield, Maryann Penczak, and Sally Leighton for their many hours of proofreading, editing, and suggestions. I am tremendously indebted to them for their time and for their interest in helping me improve this book, all for the sake of charity. Their contributions vastly improved this book. THANK YOU!

I experienced a miracle when four people who did not know me led me to discover Maddie's story—"Mysterious Medical Miracle." I would like to thank Karen Kimi Erfort, Marilyn J. Peterson, Timothy D. Peterson, the late John H. Rankin, Pat Pugh, M.D., and a very special family who will remain anonymous. I realize that there may be some other explanation, error, or mishandling that may have taken place before the technician took Maddie's X-ray that day. But none of the medical staff present had any knowledge or understanding of how this result may have occurred. To quote Maddie's mother, "It is a sweet and innocent story." It is an incredible story with or without the X-ray.

I also wish to thank two individuals who helped me with the mechanics of creating this book. First, I would like to thank my daughter, Lana, for all the hours of graphic designing and suggestions she contributed to enhance this book. Secondly, I would like to thank Scott Wagner for his help in converting Maddie's X-ray to a format that I could incorporate into my Web site and Facebook photos.

Mr. John McCullough kindly gave me a beautiful photograph he had taken of one of the most vivid rainbows I have ever seen. Although we were not able to actually use this photo, or part of this photo, it was a very helpful guide necessary in creating two very realistic rainbows for the cover. Thank you for your generosity.

I would like to thank the following people from the bottom of my heart: Diane Ayers, Lenore Kelly, Pat Kantecki, a pastor from Florida, Kathy Hoover, Holly Restemayer, Leo Larson, the late Bobby Larson, the late Virginia May, Evelyn M. Daudelin, the late Liz La Rocco, Betty Borgeson, Susan Katte, Fr. Eugene Faucher, Marcia Rau, Katie Falkenberg, Ron Madl, Christine Hardenburg, Jim Gaughn, Kathryn Marchioni Davy, H. Richard Hagen, Sally Leighton, Mary E. Jurewicz, Margaret M. Wood, Mary Bernadette Hurley, Anne Pauly, Phyllis Greco, Cecile Cunningham, Martha L. Maxson, the late

Edmund Skiba, Alieh Sadati, Rev. Paul Kelly, S.C.J., Ginger Mueller, Jolene Pasta, and all contributors who wished to remain anonymous. This book would not be possible without their stories.

I thoroughly enjoyed working with all the staff at Authorhouse Publishers over the past few years. I highly recommend this company to anyone interested in self-publishing a book.

Contents

SECTION THREE
Visions

SECTION FOUR
Out of Body Experiences

SECTION FIVE
Angels

SECTION SIX
Signs from the Deceased

SECTION SEVEN

Healing

SECTION EIGHT

Prayers That Were Answered

SECTION ONE

My Personal Stories

one

The Heavenly Voice

When I was a child, I used to speak as a child, think like a child, reason like a child; when I became a man, I did away with childish things.

— 1 Corinthians 13:11

I HAD AN AMAZING experience when I was seven years old. Unfortunately, at the time, I did not reveal it for fear that my family would think I was crazy. Now, as an adult, I finally feel comfortable sharing that experience.

When my parents divorced, my mother, younger brother, and I moved from Seattle, Washington, to Cuba City, Wisconsin, to live with her parents. The divorce became final on my first day of kindergarten. We lived with them approximately one year and then moved into an apartment in town.

My grandfather was a Methodist minister in Cuba City. Later on he was transferred to a church in Shullsburg, Wisconsin. My brother and I spent our summers with our grandparents in Shullsburg, while our mother worked just a few miles away, as a hairdresser in Cuba City.

I can remember always being a prayerful child. I prayed before bed, and my brother and I took turns praying before each meal, unless it was a Sunday or a holiday. That is when my grandfather would say grace.

One hot summer morning I was walking around the parsonage yard, bored as could be, when I heard some noise coming out of the church. Someone was cleaning. I walked over to the church and noticed that the doors of the church were wide open, which is why I could so clearly hear a pail being set down and moved around. Shullsburg was a small town. I wondered if I had ever seen the person who was inside.

I stood there looking in but was unable to focus because of the contrast between the sunlight and the dark interior of the church. I slowly walked up the cement stairs to get a closer look. My brother and I were given specific instructions to never play inside the church. We were only allowed to go inside the church when we were with our family members. (I had happy memories of my brother and me taking turns holding on to the rope as the church bell rang and being gently lifted a few feet off the floor. Of course we could only do this because my grandfather supervised and gave his permission.)

The sounds of the pail being moved around stopped. I didn't see anyone. My eyes followed the carpet down the aisle. I slowly gazed up at Jesus on the cross. At the very moment my eyes met the eyes of Jesus I heard a woman's voice say, "Give my Son some flowers." The voice was very kind and loving, and it sounded as if it was behind me, but no one was there. I thought about how much Jesus would like a nice bouquet of flowers, and I had never given Him a present.

I realized I would be in big trouble if I pulled any of my grandmother's flowers, so I dashed off to the park across the street. I knew I would be able to find a variety of beautiful flowering weeds that He would like. When I had gathered a sizable bouquet, I quietly walked into the church, deposited the flowers directly below Jesus' feet, and promptly left.

That day at lunch, my grandmother asked, "Why were you playing in the church?"

I told her, "I wasn't playing in the church. I thought that Jesus would like some flowers, so I left them in the church."

I was not in the habit of lying. This was my first lie. Why did I take full credit for this gift? Because, I knew how crazy it would sound if I told my family that a woman who wasn't there told me to give her son some flowers.

Now that I am older, I have read about the Blessed Mother appearing before and speaking to children in Fatima, Lourdes, and Medjugorje. Perhaps the innocence of children is why they have been chosen. I can only wonder how the rest of my life may have changed if I had had the courage to admit the truth when I was a child.

two

Making a Hammock

God is our refuge and strength,
a very present help in trouble.

— Psalms 46:1

MY HUSBAND AND I realized that as our family grew we would need to leave our condominium, so in 1986 we built our new home. I knew that I wanted all four of our bedrooms to have crucifixes over the doors. I felt comforted knowing that no evil would enter while we were sleeping. I encouraged our daughters to choose their own crucifixes. Fr. John Hurley blessed them for us at the Holy Thursday Dinner that year.

A couple of years later we witnessed a horrible accident. One morning my husband and I were sitting at the kitchen table drinking coffee. Suddenly, directly above our heads, we heard a loud crash. The noise was coming from our seven-year-old daughter's bedroom.

I ran upstairs to see what had happened. Lana's bedroom door was locked, so I made a mad dash for a Q-tip. I broke one end off as I rushed back to her door and popped the lock.

I was shocked to see her little feet sticking out from under her highboy dresser. I immediately tried to lift it and screamed for my husband's and daughter Nicole's help.

The drawers had safety latches and were falling downward, but not out of the highboy dresser. Amazingly, her head and chest were under her bed, which was next to the highboy dresser. Eventually, we were able to return the dresser to an upright position.

Lana explained that she was trying to make a hammock with a long scarf. She had tied one end of the scarf to a handle on the dresser that was to the left of her bedroom door. The other end of the scarf was tied to a handle on the highboy dresser that was along the other wall next to her bed. The door to her bedroom was at the corner of those walls. When she sat on the scarf, the highboy dresser tipped over.

We felt that we had experienced a miracle. First of all, my husband and I had different work schedules, and we were not usually home at the same time. Secondly, we cannot explain how quickly Lana could have slid her head and chest under her bed before the highboy dresser fell on top of her little body. I asked her how she got that way, and she said she didn't know. Thirdly, she did not sustain any broken bones, bruises, or scratches.

I am convinced that the Holy Spirit and angels were watching over her and protecting her as she fell under the dresser, which was just a few feet below her bedroom crucifix. That was the first miracle Lana experienced in her bedroom.

To view a photo of the highboy dresser go to:
www.touchedbythegraceofGod.com
www.facebook.com (Enter *Touched by the Grace of God* in the search window.)

three

Queen of the Baby Rosary

As one whom his mother comforts,
so I will comfort you.

— Isaiah 66:13

I̲N AUGUST 1997, A friend changed my life forever when she told me about the Queen of the Baby Rosary statues of our Blessed Mother Mary. Sometimes the statues change direction, turn their heads, light up, smell like roses, or drip oil. Our home did not have a statue of Mary, and so when I heard about the statues, I immediately wanted to get one. My friend insisted on giving me one as a present.

The statues must be ordered from Angel Kisses of St. Charles, Illinois, which is a Catholic gift shop owned by John and Patricia Kulpin. It takes two weeks for the statues to arrive. It is strongly suggested that you pray the rosary daily after you receive your statue. I thought to myself, "Oh, I can do that. I pray the rosary every day during Lent." I began to pray the rosary daily while I patiently waited for my statue of Mary. (Now I pray the rosary three times a day.)

The Blessed Mother gave Saint Dominic fifteen promises. The prayers of the rosary were given to Saint Dominic in the thirteenth century during a time when people did not pray enough. The rosary promises given to St. Dominic are listed at the end of the book.

The Queen of the Baby Rosary Statues are a little over thirteen inches tall, made of clear plastic and set on round bases, and their heads and large halos are turned slightly to the left. I like to describe them as looking like ice sculptures of Mary.

Each statue of Mary comes with a baby rosary, which has a cross and two roses on a gold cord that is covered with a few white beads. The person who receives the statue is the person who places the baby rosary necklace around the statue's neck.

I had heard stories that several people's statues had moved (changed direction), or healed people, or that the roses turned yellow and then back to pink. Some people have smelled a rose scent coming from their statues, and other people have said their statues began to glow at night, or that they began to drip an oily substance.

When I finally received my Queen of the Baby Rosary statue, I wondered if I would ever see it move. I wanted to be certain that I placed our statue in a location that would not experience any vibrations. Some people who are very devout Christians have never experienced their statues changing direction.

I kept saying the rosary daily. On the first day I studied my statue. Sometimes when you look through the back of the head you can see the face of Jesus. Only a few individuals have observed this phenomenon. There is an area near the knees where you can see the shape of an angel. This is caused by the folds of plastic on the opposite side of the statue.

When I first examined the statue and the rosary, I felt disappointed that the roses on the rosary were not full of petals, but accepted this and put it around Mary's neck. Then I studied the roses and noticed that the petals looked like they were moving! The size of the shadows changed inside the roses, as if they were breathing. I tried to hold my breath and examine the center of the roses to see if they were still moving.

It took me three days to figure out whether or not the centers of the roses were moving. I believed the roses were moving, and that is when I asked Lana to examine the roses to verify this phenomenon. Neither one of us could see movement. To this very day it has not happened again.

One month later I decided to order more statues. On September 10, 1997, I ordered five statues of the Virgin Mary with the baby rosary necklaces. I wanted one for my mother, sister, mother-in-law, a friend who had Hodgkin's disease, and a man who had been in constant pain for several years after he injured his back.

On September 27, my birthday, I went to Angel Kisses to pick up the statues and rosaries. The small store was crowded. My daughter Lana came inside the store with me. We looked around before we asked Pat to bring out the statues we had ordered.

As soon as I entered the little shop, I smelled what I thought was strong incense. It smelled similar to allspice and was so intense that it gave me a headache. When we left the shop, I asked Lana if she had smelled it too. She said she didn't smell anything. Later on, at another visit to Angel Kisses, I asked Pat about the incense, and she said they do not burn it. Pat said that if you smell a spicy smell it is the fragrance of Christ, and the scent of roses is the fragrance of Mary. During the last days of Christ's life, He was anointed with some expensive oil. The Bible tells us in Mark 14:3 that when Jesus was in Bethany at the home of Simon the leper and reclining at the table, a woman came with an alabaster jar of perfumed oil, costly genuine spikenard. She broke the jar and poured it on Jesus' head. I can't say that I know what spikenard smells like, but it caused me to wonder if it smells similar to incense or allspice.

Pat took each statue out of its box, put holy water on it in the sign of a cross, and gave it a kiss. It is at this precise moment that she finds out if a statue bows its head. If it does, she marks the box with a cross so you will know which one of your statues bowed its head.

One of our statues bowed so that it was a quarter of an inch lower than the rest of the statues. I never once felt it was for me to keep for myself. Who should receive this special statue?

At home I lined up all of the statues on the kitchen table. My entire family scrutinized them from every angle. We all agreed; they were all the same height, and only one had its head bowed. It was time to begin to give them away. This was the last time they would all be together. I felt like I was breaking up a family.

I was not able to personally deliver the statues to my mother and sister, who lived in another state, because I was not able to get away. I kept these statues in their boxes for twenty-two days, and when I was tempted to take them out and look at them, I did not.

There were two people at my church, a man and a child, with some medical problems. My heart broke for both of them, and I knew immediately that the two statues I had at home for my mother and sister should be given to them.

On October 19, I took the statues out of their boxes. I lined them up again, wanting to see them before I gave them away. I knew something was different. One of the statues was shorter! Immediately I said, "Oh my God, this one is for a child!" This statue was one quarter of an inch shorter than the others. I quizzed my family about the statues, "Were all of the statues the same height before?" Yes, we all agreed. Now one of the statues was shorter.

I took both statues to work because the woman who gave me my first statue was coming to the dental office. The wife of the man who was in constant pain was also coming in. I wanted them both to see that this statue was shorter.

My co-workers did see that the statue was shorter. What we were not expecting to see was that three hours later the head tilted to the right side. Everyone in the dental office noticed that the head changed position; by 5 p.m. it began to straighten out a little.

After work, I visited the mother of one of the people I gave a statue to earlier that week. I wanted her to see the recent changes the statues had made. She held the statue for a while and set it down while we talked. All of a sudden I noticed the back was curving. She said that she wasn't sure about that but did see that the statue was smaller and that the head had tilted to the right.

It has been several years since I gave the first statues away. How are these people doing now? One man died. One man did not experience any change; however, a few years later he felt that he was visited by an angel. I do not know the condition of the child. The man who received the statue that bowed was healed from Hodgkin's disease. My mother-in-law's statue changed position a few times during the final months of her life.

One thing I do know is that no matter what their physical outcome has been, they all felt comforted. The statues cause a deepening of faith, or a renewed interest in religion, and this may be more important than physical healing.

Over the years I have ordered many statues. I estimate that I have purchased forty-eight Queen of the Baby Rosary statues. Now I encourage others to visit the shop and purchase their own statue.

I realize that I may have spent too much time viewing the statues, hoping for some indication of unusual activity, when I originally discovered them. Now, however, almost fifteen years later, I have a lackadaisical approach to the statues. I realize what they are capable of.

Two of the most dramatic effects I had ever witnessed happened in our home while my husband and I took care of his mother, Virginia, during the final two and one half years of her life. She was completely bedridden with stage four breast cancer, which had already spread to her bones. So we equipped Lana's "miracle bedroom" with a hospital bed for Virginia.

By the time our daughter Lana married in September of 2008, we had already been caring for my mother-in-law for two years. We made arrangements for her to stay at Manor Care while we attended the wedding in Arizona. We chose to take an additional two weeks respite care when were returned. This was the only respite we had during those two years.

While she was at Manor Care, I changed the position of Virginia's hospital bed so she would have a more direct view of the television screen. She preferred to lie on her right side because it was less painful; however, this meant that she was not truly facing the screen. Amazingly, soon after, the statue of Mary moved thirty degrees towards Virginia's bed.

In February 2009, Virginia's health declined and her doctor recommended we obtain hospice assistance in our home. Virginia was very excited to be getting a "hospice" inflatable mattress. I moved some furniture to allow space for setting up the hospice hospital bed. Virginia would not be able to tolerate being suspended in a Hoyer lift. To minimize her pain, she needed to be moved to a second hospital bed. With the help of the hospice nurse and social worker, the three of us were able to transfer Virginia from one hospital bed to the other.

I moved the furniture back in place once she had been transferred to the new bed and grabbed an extension cord for the lamp. When I threw the cord over the mirror on the dresser, the statue of Mary landed face down on the carpet. Her baby rosary flew off her neck. The statue did not break.

I picked Mary up, gave her a kiss, told her I was sorry and placed her baby rosary necklace over her head. Then I took her over to my mother-in-law and said, "Give Mary a kiss. She just fell on the floor."

Virginia gave her a kiss and said, "Mary, it was just an accident." Virginia always loved Mary and had talked to her long before I was her daughter-in-law. If Mary wasn't listening she would scold her. They were very good friends.

I realized that when I placed the statue back on the dresser I would have to do it in such a way that I would notice if the statue had moved. Therefore, I decided to align the statue's shoulders with the edge of the dresser.

I left the room for twenty minutes. When I returned the statue had turned thirty degrees to face Virginia in her new bed. Mary was showing me that she was closely watching over Virginia, and I believed Mary was preparing me for my mother-in-law's impending death. That evening Virginia began to cough. The next day her breathing had a gurgling sound. Five days later she was gone.

Virginia's last five days were very peaceful. Sometimes when I would enter her room I could smell the fragrance of Christ. She was always smiling. She complained about nothing. Twice she told me groups of people were in her room. She would not tell me who they were. She told me she didn't want her mother to see her this way. Then I asked if her mother was present and she said, "No." I do not believe I had ever seen her quite this happy before. Virginia left this world on February 15, 2009.

I do not know why God would cause the statues to move. I do feel it is a mystery. It is a grace from God that I will not understand in this life, but I have experienced a stronger faith, peace and comfort because of these experiences.

You may view photos of the statues at:

www.touchedbythegraceofGod.com

www.facebook.com (Enter *Touched by the Grace of God* in the search window.)

Brochures on how to say the rosary may be obtained through:

Priests of the Sacred Heart

Sacred Heart Monastery

P. O. Box 900

Hales Corners, Wisconsin 53130

(414) 425-3383 | (800) 448-7674

poshusa.org

Angel Kisses of St. Charles

504 E. Main Street

St. Charles, Illinois 60174

(630) 377-0588

four

The Last Photograph

For our lifetime is the passing of a shadow;
and our dying cannot be deferred because
it is fixed with a seal; and no one returns.

— Wisdom 2:5 NAB

I N 1967, WHEN I was a teenager, my mother remarried. Marvin Gunnarson was an auto-body repairman and an excellent automobile painter. He was also a veteran of the Korean War.

On November 30, 1968, my little sister Holly was born. Then on December 3, 1969, Marvin adopted me and my brother Ted. The adoption would carry on the Gunnarson family name. Since Marvin supported us, the decision to adopt us always made sense to me.

I lived at home for only a few years after the adoption. My brother left home a few years later when he got married. Mom, Dad, and Holly moved to Casper, Wyoming, for a few years and then headed to Crystal, North Dakota, where Marvin grew up. There they purchased a tavern with an attached residence. The tavern was named appropriately: "Gunnar's Tavern."

Marvin always had a cough because he was a heavy smoker. When he was sixty-one years old, he found out he had lung cancer. To receive his medical treatments, he had to travel between home and Fargo, where the Veteran's Administration Hospital was located.

One weekend, when Marvin was back in Crystal visiting with some friends at Gunnar's Tavern, his friends decided to take a photograph of him and my mother sitting at the bar. At the exact moment the photograph was snapped, the camera broke. The film fell out of the camera onto the floor. Not knowing if the light had damaged any of the pictures, their friends decided to have the film developed regardless of the outcome.

The only photograph that turned out was the photograph of Marvin and my mother. That was the last photograph taken of Marvin before he died on July 27, 1987.

five

The First Time I Prayed For Myself

So Jesus said to them again, "Peace be with you;
as the Father has sent Me, I also send you." And
when He had said this, He breathed on them and
said to them, "Receive the Holy Spirit."

— John 20:21-22

THE FIRST TIME I prayed for myself was November 17, 1991. I was thirty-nine years old.

For some reason I had always felt that my prayers should be for everyone else in the world. Don't most people feel this way? We are constantly hearing about so many less fortunate people in the news who are experiencing all kinds of problems. They really need our prayers.

I felt I was one of these individuals when one weekend I felt two swollen lymph nodes under my right armpit. I was really scared. I hoped this was not going to lead to cancer. I still had a lot of living to do. I wanted to be there to help raise our daughters. How was I going to conceal my worry during Lana's birthday party, in our home, on November 25? The invitations were in the mail, and all the arrangements had been finalized.

I called a friend who had breast cancer. She was so concerned when I talked to her that she gave me her surgeon's emergency phone number and made me promise that I would call him as soon as I hung up with her.

I felt uncomfortable calling a doctor who had never seen me as a patient. I was so worried and upset that I could not give the answering service operator all the patient information he needed. I had to hang up because I was about to cry.

Within a few minutes the phone rang. It was the surgeon on call. With much concern, he asked me a few questions. I told him about the swollen lymph nodes. I told him I would call to schedule an appointment at his office once I rescheduled my patients. He told me to call his office on Monday and tell the receptionist that he said he would see me at noon.

My daughters knew about the lumps I had found, and they told me that they did not want to go to church with me on Sunday if I was going to cry. I told them that I wouldn't cry, but truthfully I was not completely positive that I really would not cry at church.

That Sunday I did a lot of things I had never done before while I was praying. Usually before the Mass began I would pray for all the problems in the world. That day was different. I looked at the crucifix and for the first time prayed with my eyes open. I said to God, "If I ever needed you, I need you now." I paused and prayed, "Come into me." I thought to myself, where did those thoughts come from?

Later that evening as I was walking our dog, tears began welling up. I was about to cry when, as I was walking past a light post, the most wonderful feeling came over me. In the blink of an eye, I was filled with joy and peace. I felt like laughing. A huge weight had been lifted from me. All my worry was gone. My prayer was answered. The Holy Spirit entered my body. I knew I was going to be all right. Now I understood the meaning of my prayer, "Come into me."

I thought about canceling my doctor appointment the next day. I knew that I was going to be all right and in a few days I was, even though I now had three swollen lymph nodes, which may have been a reaction to deodorant.

· six ·

A Visitor in the Night

Therefore I say to you, all things for which you
pray and ask, believe that you have received them,
and they will be granted you.

— Mark 11:24

WHEN OUR DAUGHTER LANA was in middle school, she developed bronchitis and allergies. Her doctor was able to address the bronchitis condition with some antibiotics, but Lana was continually experiencing nasal congestion so severe that she was unable to smell or taste.

We waited to see if she had seasonal allergies, but she wasn't any better in the winter than in the summer. On occasion, when she could breathe through her nose, she knew she would be able to taste. During these brief periods of relief, which only lasted a few minutes, she would rush down to the kitchen to eat whatever she could find.

By the time Lana was in high school her allergies were no better. Her physician sent us to an allergist. He gave us samples of medications to try, but nothing helped her. He was so surprised by this that he took a scope and looked down her nose into her throat. When the allergist saw her polyps, he suggested we see an ear, nose, and throat doctor.

The ENT doctor said that he would remove the polyps if we wanted him to but that they usually came back. Lana chose not to have the polyps removed. Instead the allergist ran a series of skin tests. The results showed that Lana was allergic to dust, grass, maple trees, oak trees, and smoke; so she began taking allergy shots.

After awhile Lana became tired of the frequent visits to the allergist's office. In fact, not only did the injections not help her, but she felt worse. She wanted to be at home studying and doing her homework. So we stopped going to the allergist.

A friend I knew insisted that I read two of her books about people who had received the wounds of Christ. The first book I read was about the life of Padre Pio.

At one point in the middle of the book, while I was reading about all the miracles of healing he performed, I thought to myself, "I wonder if Padre Pio would help my daughter?" I didn't doubt that he could do it, but I wondered if he would be allowed to do it.

That night I kept waking up. Every time I turned over I thought that I had not finished my prayers. I kept praying for Lana. All night I prayed over and over for her. Although I did not have a sound sleep, I did not wake up tired.

I was always the first one to wake up in the morning. I would unlock the front door so I wouldn't get locked out of the house when I walked the dog. Then I exercised and ate breakfast.

I was on my way upstairs to get ready for work when Lana unlocked her door to tell me this story. "Mom, there was a man in my room last night!" she excitedly exclaimed.

I could tell that she was dead serious. I thought about what she said and realized that she always locked her bedroom door at night. I wondered how this could have happened and said, "The front door was locked, the dog did not bark, I didn't hear anything during the night, and your bedroom door was locked."

Lana emphatically said, "I swear there was a man in my room last night, and he had on a brown robe."

I thought immediately of Padre Pio because he always wore a brown robe. I asked Lana, "Did you have your eyes open?"

"No!" she replied.

Curiously I asked her, "Then how did you know that there was a man with a brown robe on?"

Lana quickly answered, "I don't know. I was too scared to open my eyes. He had each of his hands on my shoulders, shaking me back and forth calling my name . . .Lana . . .Lana . . .Lana. He came into my room two times."

That morning Lana was able to breathe through her nose, smell, and taste again. Her allergies are now seasonal instead of permanent. This was Lana's second miracle.

seven

The Confirmation Dress

*Jesus said to them, "Fill the water pots with water." So they filled
them up to the brim. And He said to them, "Draw some out now
and take it to the headwaiter." So they took it to him. When the
headwaiter tasted the water which had become wine, and did not
know where it came from (but the servants who had drawn the
water knew), the headwaiter called the bridegroom, and said to
him, "Everyman serves the good wine first, and when the people
have drunk freely, then he serves the poorer wine; but you have
kept the good wine until now."*

— John 2:7-10

I N 1997, OUR DAUGHTER Lana was in the process of preparing for her
confirmation, and I knew that it was time to begin to look for the dress she
would wear that day. A dELiA*s catalog came to our home. I saw a black
dress with baby blue flowers embroidered on it that I thought she would like
because those were her favorite colors. She looked through the catalog and liked
the dress. I surprised her by ordering it on October 3.

When the dress came and Lana tried it on, it was a perfect fit except for one
thing: the dress was below her knees. The dress pictured in the catalog was just
above the knees. I was surprised to see this discrepancy.

Lana clearly did not like the longer hem. She pulled the dress up, a little too
high, to show me where she thought the hemline should be. I tried to tell her that

the shorter length was not appropriate for a confirmation dress, but I did not want to get into an argument over this. So I silently asked our Blessed Mother Mary to help me to convince Lana what the proper hem length should be.

I told Lana that when she was on her winter break and I had time off from work we would take the dress to be professionally hemmed. I did not want to attempt to hem both layers of this delicate fabric. So Lana hung the dress in her closet. It was hanging there during the time she had the visitor in the night (Padre Pio).

Another dELiA*s catalog came in the mail. Lana saw it before I did and was excited to find some shoes that she would like to wear with her confirmation dress. On November 11, I ordered the shoes.

We had the confirmation dress for approximately three weeks when the shoes finally arrived. Lana surprised me later that night by barging into my bedroom wearing her confirmation dress and new shoes.

She was beaming. When I looked at the length of the dress I could see why. The dress was three inches shorter and was the perfect length. I thanked Mary for answering my plea—to help me find the proper length for Lana's confirmation dress. This was Lana's third miracle.

To view Lana's confirmation dress and shoes go to:

www.touchedbythegraceofGod.com

www.facebook.com (Enter *Touched by the Grace of God* in the search window.)

eight

More Special than a Rainbow

But as for me, I would seek God, and I would place my cause before God; who does great and unsearchable things, wonders without number.

— Job 5:8-9

GOD EXHIBITS SOME OF His most amazing powers outside. Many of Jesus' miracles were performed outside. For example, St. Bernadette saw her visions of the Blessed Mother Mary outside in a grotto. She prayed outside. The children of Fatima saw the Blessed Mother Mary outside. The children prayed outside. The same thing happened in Medjugorje. Innocent children saw a vision of Mary, and later large numbers of people gathered to this location. Some people report that they see the sun spinning, as well as other unexplainable things.

I began to pray outside, too, whenever I walked our dog. Usually I would pray the rosary.

One evening several years ago, I took our dog out for his last walk of the day around our neighborhood park. In my peripheral vision, I could see some fog in the park. It was odd to see fog when we hadn't had any for several months. I turned my head to get another look.

I couldn't believe my eyes! Across the street in my neighborhood park was a huge dome of fog entirely positioned over the baseball diamond. None of the fog touched one blade of grass. The highest point was about ten feet high. It was as if someone turned a giant glass bowl of fog upside down on the baseball diamond. I wished someone else could have been with me to witness how God displayed His power on earth. I still needed to walk my dog. I headed two blocks north and then came back to the park—hoping I could still see the dome of fog.

It was still there! I stood there enjoying this special gift for as long as I could. Within a few minutes a small, thin section of fog came out of the creek. It was narrow and moved slowly like a snake until it connected with the dome of fog. Next I watched as the height of the dome of fog slowly condensed to about three feet high and stayed behind the border of grass along the baseball diamond. When the fog looked as if it was about knee high I walked home. I knew I had just witnessed something more special than a rainbow because I would probably never see anything like it again. I have lived in this neighborhood for more than twenty-seven years, and this was the only time a dome of fog appeared.

nine

October

And Jesus answered and said to them, "Truly I say to you, if you have faith and do not doubt, you will not only do what was done to the fig tree, but even if you say to this mountain, 'Be taken up and cast into the sea.' It will happen. And all things you ask in prayer, believing, you will receive."

— Matthew 21:21-22

For some reason, special things happen to me in October, and it seems they are connected to my first visit to Angel Kisses. Maybe it is because that's when I began to pray the rosary every day. A few of these stories are recounted below, in chronological order. Some are stories about prayers that have been answered. Others tell of unbelievable events.

Often at church we were asked to be a little more generous with our treasure. I felt that this request didn't apply to me because I already had other obligations to fulfill. I rationalized that as long as I donated my usual amount my contribution was enough. But I repeatedly heard for several weeks that more money was needed for special purposes.

I began to feel guilty when I missed my opportunity to participate in those collections. While I was at church, I prayed for another chance to donate some money. Later that afternoon a nun called my home, asking me to donate some money.

I was very surprised to have received a phone call like that. Never before had a nun called our home asking for a donation, and I have not received a call like that since. What I remember most about this is that my prayer was answered the same day.

I realized that I needed to follow the Bible lesson in Luke 16:13 about the importance of money. It says, "No servant can serve two masters; for either he will hate the one and love the other, or else he will be devoted to one and despise the other. You cannot serve God and wealth."

The next year a similar situation came up. I was not being as generous as I should have been with my money, preferring to spend it on the things I wanted rather than give it to the church. Guilt set in again. That Sunday I prayed for another chance to be generous. Not long before this, I had been trying to sell a clarinet we no longer needed. I advertised at schools and in grocery stores. No one called.

On Monday, the day after I prayed for a chance to be generous, I had a conversation with a mother who told me that her daughter wanted to take clarinet lessons but that they could not afford a clarinet. I knew immediately why my clarinet had not sold. After lunch I brought the clarinet to work and gave it to the mother.

On October 1, 2001, I had just begun a dental cleaning when I realized that one of my instruments was not on the tray. I needed my posterior curette, which is a scaling instrument for the back teeth. Instead, I had two anterior curettes, which are scaling instruments for the front teeth. I realized how this occurred. One of the anterior curettes fell into the section with the posterior curettes. Then, when I reached for one of each, I did not notice that I had picked up two anterior curettes.

I stared at the tray, trying to decide if I should place the posterior curette on the tray before my gloves became contaminated with saliva. I spent so much time trying to decide if I would use it that I am sure my patient was wondering why I was taking so long to get started. Eventually, I chose not to replace the instrument.

A few minutes into the cleaning, I realized that I needed the posterior curette. I looked at my drawer and thought about putting on a clean glove to pull out the sterile instrument. Again, I paused a long time to think about whether I could continue the cleaning without the posterior curette. Then I thought about using my cavitron, which is an ultrasonic scaler that vibrates and sprays water.

After a few more minutes of work with my cavitron, I still could not get into the area between the roots. The shape of the tooth did not allow me good access with the cavitron. I kept thinking I should get the posterior curette. Out of habit, I looked at the tray to reach for the posterior curette. **It was there!** I couldn't believe my eyes! I had just experienced a miracle! I had one of each type of dental instrument. There were no longer any duplicate instruments on the tray!

A metal instrument had been transformed on my dental tray. I am 300 percent positive of this because I paused, studied the instruments three separate times, and took plenty of time to decide whether or not to put that instrument on the tray.

I asked myself, "Why did God do this?" One month earlier we had all experienced the extreme sadness of the events that occurred on September 11, 2001. I decided that God thought that it would help me if He showed me that He would give me whatever I needed and that I could always trust Him to do that. God would provide for my needs—no matter how bad life seemed.

Several of my unusual experiences have occurred while I was walking my dog Sparky. One evening I was about one block away from home when I noticed we were being followed by a fox. I became a bit scared because my little dog looked like a nice meal to a wild fox.

There was no one else around, and the fox was definitely following us. When we stopped, the fox stopped too. I decided to turn around and go home since we had just begun our walk, but this meant that we were going to have to get closer to the fox!

Every time we stopped, the fox would look directly at us. I decided to pick up Sparky for his own safety and to facilitate our escape. I said a prayer and asked God to talk to the fox to tell him to leave us alone. I tried to hurry while carrying Sparky, but the fox was running too. I stopped near the creek across the street from my house and prayed again, asking God to please talk to the fox and tell him to let us get home. I ran for the front door. The fox ran too. He was standing in the same spot I was just standing in by the creek. He stared at us as we went through the front door. **We were safe!**

I wondered if I was overreacting to the danger I felt because the fox was following us so closely. I considered that perhaps I didn't really need God's help. Several years later, in 2008, I heard about a jogger in Arizona who was bitten by a rabid fox. She jogged one mile to her car, put the fox in the trunk of her car, and drove herself to the hospital. She and the veterinarian were bitten and received rabies vaccinations. I knew then that my fear was justified. Thank you God for protecting me and my dog!

These examples of answered prayers, physical transformation of a dental instrument, and protection have deepened my faith. We are expected to believe and trust Him without signs. I do.

ten

St. Maria Goretti Church

And Jesus said to the centurion, "Go; it shall
be done for you as you have believed."

— Matthew 8:13

URING AN OCTOBER 1987 pilgrimage to Medjugorje, some
parishioners of St. Maria Goretti parish in Scottsdale, Arizona,
experienced peace and conversion. Upon their return to the
parish, they had a strong desire to pray, fast, and experience reconciliation.
On December 3, 1987, they began a prayer group which grew to over
500 people.

In July of 1988, during the Thursday evening prayer group, Gianna Talone
began receiving messages from, and experiencing apparitions of, Our Lady. Fr.
Jack Spaulding also began to receive messages from Our Lady and Our Lord
during the homily. Our Lord would sometime speak and give messages through
one of the young adults. These messages have been written down. Fr. Jack decided
to make the messages public in August of 1989, publishing the six-volume series,
I am your Jesus of Mercy.[1]

I did not hear of any of these occurrences while they were happening. My friend
who told me about Angel Kisses also told me a very interesting story about her
friend's granddaughter with a medical problem who was healed after she went to

St. Maria Goretti Church. I also heard stories about St. Maria Goretti Church from Pat at Angel Kisses.

I knew that someday I had to go to St. Maria Goretti parish after reading the first five volumes of *I am your Jesus of Mercy* books. I found all of them to be very inspirational. I wanted to learn more about the events described in them, so I also viewed a videotape about the church. I realized that I had a chance to find the church when I took my daughters to orientation at Arizona State University over Labor Day weekend in 1998.

I was very excited, but I also had a feeling for several weeks before the trip that something bad was going to happen. During a conversation with one of my patients, I expressed this concern. She asked me if I was afraid to fly, and I told her that wasn't the reason. I didn't feel that it had anything to do with flying out there. Why did I have this feeling?

The sky was rumbling with thunder and was filled with flashes of lightning as our jet approached Phoenix. I was thinking to myself that Arizona seldom gets rain and hoped it wouldn't rain while we were there.

As soon as we picked up our rental car, we headed to the Princess Hotel in Scottsdale. The power was out when we arrived, so our room was changed to a casita because it did not use a key card.

As we unpacked our suitcases, I looked in my purse for the little card with the address of St. Maria Goretti Parish. I couldn't find it. I dumped everything in my purse onto the bed. I still couldn't find it. I knew I packed it. Where was it? I looked through everything three times, and I still could not find the card.

I thought I could look in a phone book and find the church, but I only found St. Maria Baretti Church. That wasn't it; it wasn't in the phone book. I decided to give up for the time being.

A few minutes later we were driving around looking for a restaurant. While we listened to the radio we heard the news that Princess Diana was in a car accident in Paris. Her condition was not known. I then knew that this was the bad thing I sensed was going to happen.

I never made it to St. Maria Goretti Church that weekend. When I arrived home I threw my purse on the bed, and the card with the church's address fell out. I guessed that it was not my time to go there. I had just recently found out about Angel Kisses, and I felt the Lord intended that I should have many more religious experiences before I went to St. Maria Goretti Church.

In July 1999, I began making airline and car rental reservations for another trip to Arizona. In August I would help Nicole move into one of the dorms at Arizona State University. Nicole suggested we rent a convertible because it would be easier for us to load the luggage into the car. It sounded like a good idea, so I let her talk me into making those arrangements.

A few weeks before we were to leave for Arizona, I had a very vivid dream. In the dream I was driving a white convertible and someone tried to steal it.

I looked forward to the trip and another chance to visit St. Maria Goretti Church. I couldn't wait!

It was a beautiful day when we landed. We quickly picked up our luggage and waited for Avis to bring us our car. When I saw that the car was maroon with a beige top, I mentioned to Nicole that it looked like my dream was wrong.

While we were stopped at an intersection, I thought that I could see something coming out from under the hood and asked my daughter if it was steam or dirt blowing. Before she answered, the car died. I got it started again. The same thing happened at the next light. I turned around in the Arizona Mills Mall parking lot and put the top up. We turned back in the direction of the airport. The car died again. I started it again and pulled into a gas station. I knew we could not make it back to the airport, so I called Avis and they said they would deliver another car but that it could take a while. A couple of hours later they arrived with a white convertible Eclipse.

After all of my daughter's belongings had been moved into the dorm, I had some time to myself to look for St. Maria Goretti Parish. This time I printed out a map of the location on a sheet of typing paper. I didn't think I would be able to misplace a piece of paper that size.

The church was smaller than I expected. The neighborhood was quiet and in an older part of Scottsdale. It was around 4 p.m. when I arrived, and there were a few cars parked in the lot.

I did not try to open the church doors. It seemed funny that I would travel so far and not even try to get into the church, but I didn't.

There was a bench outside; I decided to sit down and pray the rosary. I had not prayed the rosary yet that day, so this seemed like the perfect place to do this. It was very hot, and the bench was not in the shade. I asked for a special gift as I prayed the rosary that day. I prayed that my silver rosary would change color to gold. I have heard of this happening to other people. My reason for this request was to help my husband have a stronger faith.

Two days later, in the morning, someone attempted to steal the car while it was parked near one of the dorms. The passenger side keyhole had been punched in. The door and the window did not work. My dream did happen! I had three rental cars in four days.

One month later, during the evening, I was looking through my jewelry box. I moved some items around, including a large silver cross necklace that my husband had given me. The cross is about two inches long. It is on a velvet type of cord instead of a chain. I hardly wore it because it seemed so large. Something looked different about it that evening. It didn't seem to shine the same as usual. I put it directly into a bright light. Oh my God! It had turned gold.

I immediately showed it to my husband. He made a joke about it. He said we should sell it now that it was gold. Pat from Angel Kisses told me that I prayed for the wrong thing. I should have prayed for his conversion or that God's will be done. It was a good lesson for me.

Since then several of my rosaries, holy medals, and crucifixes have partially turned gold. I have given away most of these holy medals.

My most recent experience with holy medals changing color happened October 20, 2008. On that day, one of my patients gave me a Medjugorje holy medal from a recent trip she and her husband made to Yugoslavia. The medal partially turned gold before Christmas that year.

God also tested me with my request. He turned some of my favorite silver jewelry half gold too. I was a little angry the first time I noticed my favorite silver necklace and silver watch had begun to turn gold. I immediately said to myself, "Hey, that's what you asked for." I have accepted this and now it doesn't matter. We should not be obsessed with our material possessions. They are not what is truly important.

A few years ago I met a woman, named Lois, who told me that in 1996, she and her husband took a trip to Scottsdale, Arizona. They went to a Mass at St. Maria Goretti Church. Fr. Jack Spaulding said the Mass that morning. Lois said, "At the end of the homily, Fr. Spaulding spoke to the congregation about the Gospel. In a deeper profound voice that I cannot describe, and one which we will never forget, Fr. Spaulding said, '**Remember, I love you!**' I can still hear it in my mind after all these years. We both looked at each other in a questioning way, knowing something was different. We both experienced a chilling sensation. The words were very articulate and loving."

— *Lois*

Photos of St. Maria Goretti Parish may be viewed at:
www.touchedbythegraceofGod.com
www.facebook.com *(Enter Touched by the Grace of God* in the search window.)

[1]Permission given by Queenship Publishing, *I am your Jesus of Mercy*, Vol. 1. 1989, iv-v.

eleven

Give Me a Positive Sign

*Jesus said to him, "Because you have seen
Me, have you believed? Blessed are they
who did not see, and yet believed."*

— John 20:29

M Y FATHER-IN-LAW, TEDDY, DIED on October 9, 1999. The evening
after the funeral, my husband Dan kept saying that he wanted
a positive sign from his father Ted or his uncle Frank (who died
September 19, 1997), that there is someplace we go after we die. He talked
about this for about a half hour, saying that he did believe in heaven, but he
wanted a positive sign.

The next morning he asked me if I remembered that he wanted a positive sign.
I said, "Yes."

Then he said that at the time he was talking about a positive sign, his watch
stopped working. I thought that might be a sign. He said, "No, it is not a
positive sign."

I thought it was unusual that his watch would stop working since we had just
replaced the battery only a couple months before. I told him I would look for the
receipt so we could get the battery replaced, but by the time I found it his watch
had already begun to work again.

Our daughter, Nicole, was attending Arizona State University at the time of her grandfather's death. We did not have her come home for the funeral. She told us that on the day of grandpa's death, her bedroom clock fell off the wall and broke. I talked about this with my husband to see if this was the sign he was looking for. He said, "No, it is not a positive sign."

A short time after the funeral, my mother-in-law Virginia told us that before Teddy died, he told her to give Danny an old railroad pocket watch that he had in a glass display case. He wanted him to have the watch since they were both railroad employees. My father-in-law was not sick at this time; however, a few weeks earlier he had been in the hospital. I asked my husband if he thought that this was a sign. He said, "No, it is not a positive sign."

About two weeks later, while we were all asleep, our smoke alarm went off, waking up my husband and me. I got up to check it out. I didn't smell any smoke. The alarm stopped by itself after I was out of bed. I went back to bed.

The next day I came home at noon to have lunch with Dan. He prepared lunch as he usually does. We ate, chatted, watched television, and then left for work. Luckily, our daughter Lana came home before she went to her after-school job. When she opened the door she could smell that something was burning. She went into the kitchen and found one of the gas burners on the stove was still lit from lunch. She shut it off.

I asked my husband if he thought this was a positive sign. He didn't say anything. He doesn't ask for a positive sign anymore.

twelve

You Will Be Protected

For He will give His angels charge concerning you. To guard you in all your ways. They will bear you up in their hands, that you do not strike your foot against a stone.

— Psalms 91:11 12

O VER THE COURSE OF the past few years, on several occasions, I have felt that God's presence was protecting me. Here are a few of those stories.

One evening, I was driving home from Angel Kisses on Highway 53 during rush hour. I was listening to my rosary tapes as I approached the north entrance ramp off Northwest Highway. Traffic was bumper to bumper, but three cars were driving on the ramp at full speed. I was in the right lane, and it looked like I was on a collision course with one of those cars.

I knew I had to change lanes, but when I looked in the mirrors I knew there was nowhere to go. I tried to speed up, but couldn't, because I could only drive as fast as the cars ahead of me. If I slowed down I ran the risk of running into one of those three cars.

All of a sudden, **my steering wheel began to pull to the left**. I thought, "Oh, my God, what a time to have a problem with my steering wheel." Now I had to worry about hitting a car in the middle lane. I grabbed the steering wheel with both hands but could **not** stop the car from turning into the center lane. Desperately, I tried to control the car.

I looked in the mirrors again and noticed that there was an opening big enough for more cars in the center lane. Someone in the middle lane was driving cautiously in order to allow cars in the right lane to merge with the traffic.

When my car was centered in the middle lane, the pulling on my steering wheel stopped. I was back in control. There is no doubt in my mind that I had experienced some type of heavenly intervention. I never experienced this problem with my car again and did not feel it necessary to see a mechanic.

One evening, about nine years ago, my husband and I received a phone call from one of our daughter's friends at Arizona State University. He informed us that Nicole had broken both of her arms while she was roller blading. Her left elbow was fractured but did not need a cast. Her right arm was in a full cast.

I felt so helpless. Nicole was in pain and I wanted to be with her, but it was impossible for me to be there. While I waited for more phone calls from her friends at the hospital, I could imagine for the first time the pain and helplessness Mary must have felt as she watched her son die by crucifixion.

With the help of my daughter's friends, and the family of her college roommate, Nicole adjusted to her temporary one-armed life. After some time, she recovered enough that, with some assistance, she was able to fly home to spend Thanksgiving with us.

Thanksgiving passed, but the memory of Nicole's accident was still fresh when I slipped on some newly fallen snow, which covered a patch of ice. The instant I lost my footing, I started falling; but I was falling in slow motion. I remembered Nicole telling me she braced her fall with her arms, so I raised my hands over my head. Then my body somehow turned sideways. As I lay on the ground, I felt no pain and had no bruises. I knew at that moment why some people believe they have a guardian angel watching over them. This experience helped me realize I will be protected even when I am unaware of impending danger. There is so much peace when you trust God to always take care of you.

One of the times I felt protected from danger was on an evening when I was home alone. I had just finished washing some dishes. On one side of the sink was soapy dish water. The other side of the sink had clean dishes.

I was making some pasta, which had just finished boiling and needed to be drained. I decided to pour the water into a small area between the drying dishes in the front right corner of the sink. I assumed I would be able to aim the water into that small area.

I turned the pan so the lid would face me and I would be able to see where the water was draining. I tilted the lid on the pan slightly and slowly poured the water into the sink. Suddenly, the lid slipped and scalding water began flowing. I couldn't believe what I witnessed next! The water hit what appeared to be an invisible wall and rose up the wall as it escaped from the pan. Then the water flowed to the sides of the invisible wall and, finally, to the floor, completely missing me. I was so astonished by what I was seeing that I kept pouring the water, long after I should have stopped.

Several months later I was making pasta. I felt very confident that I would be able to drain the water between the drying dishes. I held the lid firmly as I carefully poured the boiling water with the lid facing me. I wanted to prove to myself that when the lid slipped previously, it was just an accident. The weight of the water suddenly caused the lid to slip. Again the water hit an invisible wall, rose up the invisible barrier, and fell to the sides of the wall completely missing my stomach!

You cannot experience this type of grace from God without having it change your life forever. In Luke 4:12, Jesus said to the devil when the devil was trying to trick Him, "It is said, that you shall not put the Lord your God to the test." I am not going to do this again. I do not want God to think that I am testing Him.

On April 25, 2001, I drove to Columbia City, Indiana, to begin packing my mother's belongings. She was moving into a nursing home where my sister worked as a nurse. That was also the day my mother was diagnosed with colon cancer. The cancer had spread to five places in her liver and two places in her lungs. She was beyond any life-saving treatment. All that could be done was to keep her comfortable.

When I made it home later that evening, I had an overwhelming feeling that something bad was going to happen to me on my trip back to Indiana the following weekend. I didn't mention this premonition to anyone. My friends and relatives repeatedly told me to be careful. One of my co-workers even offered to loan me her cell phone. I almost said yes, and wanted to tell her of my intuition, but I decided not to. I did not even mention anything to my husband because I knew he would say that my expectations might actually cause something bad to happen.

I decided against leaving for Indiana after work on Saturday afternoon because I would hit a lot of traffic. Instead, I decided to leave at 5:30 a.m. on Sunday morning.

I went to Mass on Saturday since I would not be able to attend Mass on Sunday. I prayed for protection on my trip but nothing else.

That evening before I went to bed I prayed, "Please protect me on my trip." I repeated that prayer again at 5:00 a.m. before I got out of bed. I dreaded leaving. I actually left for Indiana at 5:35 a.m. I delayed leaving, thinking that I might avoid what I feared was going to happen to me. Then I realized that delaying my departure could have the opposite effect and make the situation worse. So I left for Indiana immediately.

I wondered what was going to happen. Would I have a flat tire? I had never had a flat while I was driving. What would that feel like? How would I be able to handle the car? Would I have an accident? I had never had a car accident. A lot of things could happen during the six hour round trip. I knew, however, that God would protect me in my car just as he did on my trip home from the Angel Kisses store.

Just west of Valparaiso, Indiana, I was stopped at a traffic light and had just finished listening to my rosary tapes. Before the light changed, I noticed that cars coming over the hill heading west were driving even with each other. The two lead cars were holding up the cars behind them. It appeared strange to me, and I couldn't figure it out.

When the light changed, I proceeded cautiously. I was in the left lane of a divided highway. The car in the right lane was also moving slowly. For a short time we were both going the same speed. I gradually increased my speed. In my rearview mirror I could see that the cars were continuing to stay back.

When I looked at the road ahead of me, I saw a deer in my lane looking back at me. As soon as I saw the deer, I recalled the premonition. But then I was filled with peace and I knew that I was going to be fine. I didn't even experience the adrenaline rush one gets when danger is imminent.

I decided to stay on the road even if it meant I would hit the deer. I began to brake but not too hard because for some reason I thought that brakes could overheat, fuse to the metal, and then fail. I needed to continue my trip, and this would only be possible if I had functioning brakes. I started to go into the right lane when I saw another deer coming up the center of the divided highway. As the car approached the deer, I closed my eyes to protect against broken glass if I hit the deer. I couldn't believe that I hadn't hit the deer yet. I opened my eyes. The deer was going into the right lane too! It looked as though my car hadn't moved any closer to the deer during the time I had my eyes shut. It was as if time stood still!

I panicked! I stopped braking, increased my speed, and started moving back to the left lane.

One deer hit the passenger headlight. The other deer stayed between the divided highway. I slowed down but did not stop. I looked in my rearview mirror and saw that the cars behind me were pulling off the road and stopping. The deer was hobbling away, its back right leg obviously injured. I couldn't understand why all of those people were stopping. The deer was not dead. I couldn't help the deer and neither could they. I kept going. I drove a short distance, trying to remember if there was any law dealing with hitting a deer. I knew not to leave an accident, but no person or car was involved here. I pulled over and looked at my car. Immediately, I could tell that the right headlight was loose. Then I saw a gas station and headed for it.

When I pulled into the gas station I was a little shaken up, so the attendant called the police. A little later I saw a squad car race past the gas station to the location where I hit the deer. When I noticed the squad car leave the accident scene, the attendant called the police again. This time I spoke directly to the police dispatcher and was advised to go directly to the police station.

I circled the police station and parked across the street. A police officer was coming out of the building as I was going up the stairs. He asked whether I was the person who hit the deer. When I replied that I was, he told me that for insurance purposes he'd have to assess the damage and complete some paperwork. He also mentioned that hitting a deer was only considered to be an incident.

I stood in front of my car while the officer examined the car. He concluded that only the headlight was affected. Later I found out that it still worked. **There was no body damage to the car! God had answered my prayers!**

The police officer told me three times how lucky I was. I felt the need to tell him that I wasn't lucky that day but rather that God had answered my prayers. I wondered whether our paths had crossed because I was supposed to encourage him to pray, but I resisted the urge to say something. There was a lesson here—that I should talk about God whenever the opportunity arises.

When you read the Bible, you encounter many amazing stories. For example, Moses was given powers to perform many astonishing feats: change a staff to a serpent; turn water to blood; cover Egypt with frogs and insects; create a plague of hail, boils, and locusts; bring darkness over the land; cause death to the first born in Egypt; and part the Red Sea. Daniel was protected in the lion's den. Shadrach, Meshach, and Abed-Nego were protected in a furnace of blazing fire. Jesus changed water to wine; multiplied bread and fish to feed multitudes of people; healed lepers, the blind, the deaf, the lame, and the paralyzed; and brought the dead back to life. Jesus may not be here physically, but the power of the Holy Spirit is all around us. God still exhibits unexpected wonders of His grace. We should not be surprised if He takes control of our cars, protects us when we slip, saves us from boiling water, or rescues us in car accidents!

Copies of the incident report and insurance documents may be viewed on:
www.touchedbythegraceofGod.com
www.facebook.com (Enter *Touched by the Grace of God* in the search window.)

thirteen

My 2004 Visit to Angel Kisses

Love justice, you who judge the earth; think of the Lord in
goodness and seek Him in integrity of heart; because He is found
by those who test Him not, and He manifests Himself to those
who do not disbelieve Him.

— Wisdom 1:1-2 NAB

I TOOK ANOTHER TRIP to Angel Kisses on the last Wednesday of October 2004. Since it is a one hour drive each way, and I did not want to make the trip by myself, I asked my friend Silvia if she would like to come with me. She agreed. Silvia and I both said a prayer at the altar as soon as we arrived. Next, we visited with Pat and John as we looked around the shop.

The altar at Angel Kisses has many statues of Jesus and Mary, some of which must not be touched. Some of the statues change direction; others may raise their arms or turn their heads. Sometimes, terminally ill customers are permitted to hold one of the original six Queens of the Baby Rosary statues.

The Sacred Heart of Jesus is positioned in the center of the statues. His arms are outstretched with a rosary draped across His hands. The heart protrudes from the body, as is the case with all statues of the Sacred Heart of Jesus. You are allowed to touch this statue's heart, and some people who do feel it beating.

The first time I was at Angel Kisses I thought I felt the heart beating, but I wasn't sure. More likely than not, I felt my pulse against the statue because there would be no doubt otherwise.

While I talked with Pat I watched Silvia pray while she touched the Sacred Heart of Jesus statue. Soon she came over to tell us that she felt the heart beating. Her excitement was obvious. Then we all noticed that the rosary was moving. Silvia said that she didn't touch it, and since I had been watching the entire time I knew this was true. The rosary was still swinging. If the rosary had been touched, it would have started moving quickly and then slowed down. This rosary was doing the opposite.

Next, Pat told us a story about a little boy who came into the shop a few days earlier. He was looking at the Sacred Heart of Jesus novena cards. The little boy was holding one of the cards between his hands like he was praying. He said he could feel the heart beating between his hands.

So Pat brought the card over to me to hold. She said, "Put it between your hands as if you are praying." I could instantly feel the heart beating and was thrilled. Silvia said she could also feel the heart beating from the novena card.

Then Pat went behind the counter and brought out a black and white 8˝ x 10˝ photo of Jesus outstretched on a cross. The background was black, and you could not see the cross. His body was so extensively bruised that it began at His neck and continued to His wrist and ankles. The bones in His right knee were visible. If this photo were in color it would have been more graphic that the crucifixion of Jesus in the movie *The Passion of the Christ*.

Pat said, "Put the picture between your hands as if you are praying." As soon as I did, I could feel the heart beating. It was so strong that I could not keep the lower part of my palms together. My hands were being pushed apart with each beat. It was awesome! Silvia also felt the heart beating when she held the photo.

I have told many people about that visit to Angel Kisses. It was such a powerful and memorable experience that I wish everyone could encounter it one day.

fourteen

The White Petunia

So then neither the one who plants nor the one who
waters is anything, but God who causes the growth.
— 1 Corinthians 3:7

O N AUGUST 8, 2002, after returning from another trip to Angel Kisses, I took my dog, Sparky, out for a walk. As I walked to the front door of our home I noticed a white petunia, which had not been there a few hours earlier.

The flower was growing through some rocks in a location where we had never planted any flowers. Twice when I pulled weeds that summer I noticed a stem shooting up through the rocks, but it didn't look like a weed so I didn't pull it. This was unusual for me because I always pull grass out if it is growing in the wrong place. This was the first time in sixteen years that I let a plant grow that we did not plant. My husband saw the stem too and decided to let it grow. We never discussed it; he just let it grow.

When I saw the petunia, I knew that it was a sign from my mother. The next day would be the first anniversary of her death, and this was her way of letting me know she was fine.

I took a picture of the flower and intended to bring it into the house before the first frost, but I was too late. I couldn't keep the flower growing, but I did save some of the seeds and planned on giving some to my brother and sister.

My daughters said that a bird probably dropped a seed there and it grew. Though I agreed with them I commented, "But look how God planned for the flower to bloom in time for the anniversary of my mother's death!"

The next year a portulaca grew in the same location. It was similar to other flowers that we grow in our yard, and they come up every year on their own. The portulaca seeds look like grains of pepper. To think that a seed that small landed in the same part of our yard and flowered for the second anniversary of my mother's death was absolutely amazing!

We removed a tree from that area, which uprooted the portulaca seed. So, on the third anniversary of my mother's death there was no flower in that location. However, in June, two months earlier than expected, a flower grew by the side of our home. It bloomed just in time for what would have been my mother's birthday.

In August of 2005, the fourth anniversary of my mother's death, a third type of flower grew in the same location as the first two in our front yard. This was a reminder from my mother that she was near.

In the spring of 2006, I had already begun my flower watch around our home, but I didn't see any. I mentioned this to my husband, and he said that he was pulling them out of the ground if they were growing in the wrong location. I asked him to stop doing that.

It appeared we would not get a birthday flower that year because no flowers were growing in the front yard, which I now call the Holy Ground.

At the same time, my daughter Lana and my future son-in-law Darryl began to build a home in Gilbert, Arizona. Mortgage interest rates were going up, so they asked to have an earlier closing date. The new closing date was scheduled for June 15, my mother's birthday, and I sensed this was a good omen.

My daughter and her fiancée approved the landscaping, and the next day they closed on their home. They immediately began to move some of their belongings, and that's when I received a phone call that there was a purple flower in their front yard. That flower had still been a bud when they did their walk-through on June 14. It bloomed on mom's birthday!

My husband told me we had one too, and he showed me a flower in our front yard directly in front of the downspout. This flower was also purple with a yellow center. Purple was my mother's favorite color.

To see two photos of the flowers that appeared in our yard go to:

www.touchedbythegraceofGod.com

www.facebook.com (Enter *Touched by the Grace of God* in the search window.)

fifteen

My Breast Cancer

In the day of my trouble I shall call upon
You, for You will answer me.

— Psalms 86:7

L ATE IN THE EVENING of April 30, 2002, I was reading my prayer card to the Sacred Heart of Jesus. Sometimes I would doze off and need to keep starting over. When I got to the passage that read, "Protect me in the midst of danger," my reading was interrupted by a male voice that said, "The worst is yet to come." I felt this was a warning but didn't know if it was a worldwide or a personal warning. My heart jumped when I heard the ominous words. Then I realized that, no matter what was going to happen, I would trust the Sacred Heart of Jesus to protect me.

I told my parish priest about the disturbing words I heard and that I thought it might be a prediction of a worldwide disaster. He suggested, however, that this might be a prediction of a personal danger. I told him that, in either case, I would place my trust in the Sacred Heart of Jesus.

In May I flew to Arizona for our daughter Nicole's college graduation. On Mother's Day, during the flight home, I experienced a line of burning pain in my left breast.

When I arrived home I examined the area and discovered three lumps. I said to myself, "Oh, my God, I have breast cancer!" I usually examine myself five times a week for breast cancer. I know positively that May 12 was the day I got the lumps and that they were not there that morning.

You would think that I would have called the doctor immediately, but I did not. A part of me did not want to know if I had breast cancer. I had to psyche myself up for the news.

I attempted to make an appointment to see my family doctor in June, but he was on vacation. I finally saw the doctor on July 7. I told him the replacement hormones he put me on four months earlier were causing some unusual bleeding. Then I described the lumps I found. He felt them and told me I had fibrocystic breasts. My friends who have fibrocystic disease described it to me, and I doubted I had this.

I told the doctor that I wanted to have a mammogram of my left breast.

He said, "You just had one." (That was on February 27.)

I said, "Yes, but I didn't have any lumps then."

Then he replied, "Things don't happen that fast."

I said, "I will pay for it. My insurance doesn't have to know about it."

My doctor said, "That is not the point. You will be receiving more radiation." He changed my replacement hormones, but he did not approve another mammogram of my left breast.

One week later a new and potentially serious problem surfaced. I discovered I had an extremely tender lymph node on my upper inside right leg near my torso. I forced myself to touch it, even though it was a huge lymph node and very painful. I called the doctor to tell him about the swollen lymph node and to let him know that I was not going to take any more replacement hormones. (Ironically, the subsequent week the television news, newspapers, and magazines were filled with reports linking replacement hormones to breast cancer.) The doctor didn't believe there was a relationship between the two, and he was right. A few weeks later I agreed with his conclusion because I realized that I accidentally caused this problem by applying fingernail polish remover along a swollen and infected portion of my right toenail. My lymph nodes were reacting to those chemicals.

In the meantime, swollen lymph nodes were now appearing all over my entire body. Within three weeks all of my lymph nodes had enlarged.

I called my family physician's office only to find out that he was on vacation again. That is when I decided to research the Internet, and I found out that acute lymph nodes, though extremely sensitive, are not cancerous. The less painful, chronic lymph nodes are most likely a result of cancer. I chose not to go to the emergency room since the lymph nodes had probably run their course.

Eventually the lymph nodes returned to normal size, but I had constant pain on the right side of my neck. I massaged the area regularly, took hot showers, and slept with a heating pad for several months. Aspirin provided relief, but I didn't want to take it indefinitely. No matter what I tried, the pain remained and my work contributed to the discomfort.

Next I made an appointment with my gynecologist. I told him about the replacement hormones, the unusual bleeding, the lumps, and the swollen lymph nodes. He was unable to find any lumps, but his assistant found them quickly. He agreed with the other doctor and said I had fibrocystic breasts, but I believed otherwise. The gynecologist said he had patients who had been taking replacement hormones for over eighteen years and didn't have any problems. He also mentioned that maybe I was not in menopause, before telling me that he was not a "lymph node man." The next day I had a procedure in his office to rule out any other problems. Everything checked out fine. Something was telling me to go to another doctor, but I began to doubt myself and decided to wait until my next physical.

On March 23, 2003, about nine months after I found the first lumps, I had my annual mammogram. I mentioned to the technician that I discovered some lumps last year but couldn't get a doctor's approval for another mammogram. I asked the radiologist to look closely at the 3 o'clock position on the left breast.

Within minutes more views were ordered. I tried to hide my worry while I waited for the results. I sensed the other patient waiting in the reception area noticed my fear. After a few more minutes I was told I should see a surgeon for a needle biopsy. I cried while I was getting dressed. As soon as I composed myself, I left.

My husband was still home when I got there. I told him everything that happened at the hospital. He told me the doctor's office called and left a message.

I returned the call and was given the name and number of a surgeon I should see. I thanked the nurse but told her I would probably see the surgeon who had examined me previously for some swollen lymph nodes.

During lunch, my husband suggested that if I went to the surgeon's office and made the appointment in person they might be able to see me today. I thought it was a good idea.

Within a short time I arrived at the surgeon's office and had secured his last appointment of the day. However, I first had to pick up my mammogram X-rays for the surgeon.

I rushed to the hospital, retrieved the mammograms, and returned to the surgeon's office to see him. As I waited in the exam room, I was completely filled with *peace* and realized that I was going to be fine. I was so relaxed that I thought I might fall asleep, even though I could still feel the pain in my neck.

When I saw my surgeon, I felt very confident knowing that he was quite an experienced and thorough surgeon. He said, "So you still remember me!"

I answered, "And you still remember me!" While he looked at the X-rays, I told him about the lumps, the hormones, and what the other doctors had said. The nurses brought in the ultrasound machine, and the surgeon began performing the ultrasound. I noticed how serious his expression was.

He finally said, "I don't see what the radiologist was looking at. I can't do a needle biopsy."

My heart sank. I was thinking to myself, "Oh, not again."

Then he continued, "You need a stereotactic biopsy in the hospital." He began to explain the procedure to me, and I could see in my surgeon's face that he could tell I had breast cancer. However, he never revealed this to me. The nurse gave me information about the stereotactic biopsy procedure and scheduled it for Wednesday, March 26.

The week of the biopsy our troops surrounded Baghdad, Iraq, and our generals were predicting the worst was yet to come. I remembered the voice I heard while I was reading my novena to the Sacred Heart of Jesus. I thought it ironic that the world was in turmoil at the same time I would find out whether or not I had cancer. The voice's words proved to be prophetic.

The news coverage that week focused on some female prisoners of war. One of those prisoners was Shoshana Johnson. I saw the look of fear on her face and began to pray for her safety, feeling that she was in more danger than I was.

The day of the biopsy arrived. The procedure was similar to being trapped in a mammogram machine for forty-five minutes, except that I was lying face down in a specialized table. I couldn't imagine staying in this position for that long unless I focused on something else. I decided to pray the rosary for Shoshana Johnson. I had more than enough time to say the entire rosary, but I said it so slowly that I never completed it.

Two days later, on Friday, I called the doctor's office to find out the results. When the doctor was too busy to call early in the day, I knew I was going to get bad news. The surgeon called and gave me the diagnosis. I had intraductal carcinoma in situ. I was in shock even though I expected the worst.

I cried at work. One of my co-workers wanted to know what was going on. I told her that I would probably feel like talking about it on Monday. I continued crying at home that evening. My eyes were so red that I did not want to attend the stations of the cross at church. I stayed home and said my own.

I began drinking small drops of holy water from Angel Kisses. This holy water was particularly special because it came from shrines of Fatima, Lourdes, Our Lady of Knock, Tears of Our Lady, Betania, Venezuela (where the host bleeds), Medjugorje, and Relic of St. Ann. The water is very pure and if kept refrigerated it is drinkable.

My surgeon wanted to talk to me that weekend. He had rounds to make at the hospital on Saturday, so he asked me to meet him there after I finished work. Later that afternoon I found out what the next steps were to my recovery: I needed a lumpectomy but would first have to meet with a radiation oncologist and a second oncologist. It was really beginning to sink in, and that caused more tears. However, the cancer was in a very early stage, stage zero, which is considered precancerous. I considered that someone with a more advanced cancer would gladly switch places with me. I held my tears back as I was leaving the hospital, but I cried while driving home.

I put my name in the prayer basket at church the first chance I had. I also asked God to guide my doctors. Every weekend approximately three thousand people would be praying for us. I saw my parish priest the same day and told him about the cancer. I told him that it was all in God's hands and that I would accept whatever He had planned for me. My priest made arrangements to give me the anointing of the sick, which I had never received. We prayed together, and I told God that when this experience was over I wanted to be one of His most holy servants. I also wanted to show appreciation for my husband's kindness and to never take him for granted. Next my parish priest asked me if I wanted to be prayed for during the Mass when we pray for the sick, and I told him I did.

I made arrangements for my lumpectomy. It was as if the appointments were being reserved for me. I got the last opening in my surgeon's schedule that week before he left for vacation. I also got the last opening in the hospital's schedule for operations. Finally I got the last opening for preadmission screening at the hospital.

That next Sunday, as the priest began to walk into church, I could smell the fragrance of Christ. I have smelled this several times since my first visit to Angel Kisses. It smells like allspice. I don't smell it that often, so I wasn't expecting it to happen. The fragrance of Christ came to me three times during the Mass that Sunday. I was being reminded that Christ was with me during this challenging time, and I felt comforted.

The next day I received mail from the Mundelein Seminary. When I opened the envelope, I could smell the fragrance of Christ. There was still time for me to request their prayers before my surgery, so I sent them a donation.

A few days later I received another envelope from the Mundelein Seminary confirming my donation. When I opened it, I could smell the fragrance of Christ. This was another reminder that He would be by my side.

Friday April 5, before leaving home for the hospital, I made the sign of the cross with my Angel Kisses' holy water across the area where I had the biopsy. Then my husband and I left for Northwest Community Hospital.

My surgeon told me that if the cancer looked like it had spread I would need a second surgery. I nodded my head, indicating that I understood him. Then I told him that if he had some extra time during surgery I would also like to have a tummy tuck.

The last thing I saw before I was sedated was my surgeon's smiling face. When I woke up, the first thing I saw was also his smiling face. He told me to come to the office on Monday, and one of his partners would remove my stitch.

That following Monday I was anxious to have my stitch removed and hear the results of the pathology report. The surgeon scheduled that day first read the biopsy report and then the pathology report. He reread them before he revealed the results. He said, "I don't think I have ever seen this before. All of your cancer was removed during your biopsy. There was no cancer found in your lumpectomy."

Happily, I thought to myself, "Wow! That is exactly what I hoped would happen!" None of the twenty-three slides showed any evidence of cancer.

I was previously told that I did not need to receive chemo. I met with the radiation oncologist and later talked to my surgeon to discuss whether I should have radiation. Most women elect to have radiation. I decided against this, even though my oncologist preferred I do radiation. However, I would have to take tamoxifen for five years and adhere to a schedule of follow-up appointments.

The Saturday evening before Easter, just before I went to bed, I was thinking how much the holy water had helped my cancer. I decided to put some on my aching neck. This was going to be a test of my faith. The **Triduum** is the holiest time of the year. (Lent is my favorite time of the year.) If I really believed I could be healed, then I would be healed. I wet two fingers and then made the sign of the cross where the pain was. I looked toward the heavens and said, "Lord, if it is in Your will, would You please take this pain away." The pain was gone before my neck was dry. **Praise the Lord! I have been cancer free for more than nine years!**

sixteen

The Dedication Page

Whatever you ask in My name, that will I do, so
that the Father may be glorified in the Son. If you
ask Me anything in My name, I will do it.

— John 14:13-14

O N AUGUST 4, 2004, I started my project by examining various books to determine what needed to be included at the front of the book. Having gathered the information I needed, I began in earnest to write the book. First, I reserved pages for the preface and acknowledgments, typing nothing more on each page than the appropriate centered heading. Then, I proceeded to draft the dedication page.

I had already chosen to dedicate the book to unbelievers. As I began writing, I decided that the page would only contain the text of the dedication; there would be no "Dedication" heading. So I started typing a few words and then pressed the enter key. To my surprise, the words centered on the page. Then I remembered I had not set the alignment to flush left. For the time being, however, it didn't matter where the words appeared on the page. I could always change the layout or words.

The next day was Wednesday. I enjoy attending weekday Masses because the turnout is so low that it almost feels like a private Mass. The first thing I did when I arrived at church that morning was pray. I prayed, "Dear God. I started the book, but You already know that. I am not a writer. So I really need Your help. Please guide me." Within five minutes I received a vision.

I could no longer see the two priests concelebrating the Mass. What I saw next was a giant layout of the dedication page the way I had typed it the day before. Then the words began to spin very quickly in all directions. When the spinning stopped, there were more words and they were in the shape of a cross. I thought to myself, "So this is what You were trying to get me to do! I'll do it!" Later that day I changed the original dedication page.

A few months later, one of my patients pointed out that the dedication appeared negative. She suggested I dedicate the book to all of God's children, which includes the unbelievers. Doing this would also set a positive tone. Now I understand why the words were spinning around in the vision and that words needed to be changed as well as added.

Special Graces

seventeen

World War II Reunion

Look at the birds of the air, that they do not sow, nor reap
nor gather into barns, and yet your heavenly Father feeds
them. Are you not worth much more than they?

— Matthew 6:26

I N JANUARY 1944, I was assigned to the 19th Cavalry Reconnaissance
Squadron and a mobile command post, which was attached to, and drawn by,
a large half-track unit. I left my home, my wife, and my two-year-old son to
serve in the military for two years. We crossed the Rhine River and entered Trier,
Germany. The right front wheel struck a land mine as we were going between the
command post and the half-track. Fortunately for me, I was thrown to the right
and sustained only a right leg injury. Many others were not that fortunate. It still
brings tears to my eyes as I remember that day.

When I was told that I could rest after this injury, I asked for permission
to spend time with my brother, Chester, who was in London, where it was
considered to be safer. Chester was in the U.S. Air Force for three years. He was
an assistant ground chief, a mechanic on B-17 bombers. He was in the 100th
Bomb Group known as the "Bloody 100." He spent two years and four months
of his duty in England.

When I arrived in England, I was to meet Chet in the Selfridge Department
Store. But it was late, the place was jammed, and I didn't find him. So I left the

store to find a place to stay. While in the room, I heard a loud explosion. The next morning I went back to the store and saw that the store's front entrance had been hit by a bomb. There was serious damage, injuries, and even fatalities. So much for England as a "safer" place!

I had no idea what had happened to my brother who was supposed to have met me at the store. I went to a nearby church to pray. While I knelt praying, I looked to my right and saw my brother, Chet, coming up next to me. I couldn't believe we found each other and neither of us had been injured. What a miracle!

— *the late Edmund Skiba*

eighteen

God Surely Has a Plan

*For we are His workmanship, created in Christ
Jesus for good works, which God prepared
beforehand so that we would walk in them.*

— Ephesians 2:10

I AM INVOLVED WITH Christ Renews His Parish-Women's Retreat. We meet on a weekly basis. Before my son's wedding I was upset because I couldn't find a dress. I mentioned this to my friends at the meeting. One of the women suggested they pray for me. I resisted, thinking there are so many more important things to pray for. But these women are persistent; we ended up praying for a dress for me.

I had planned to shop at a certain shopping center that day. However, my plans changed because we had an out-of-town guest call us to meet for lunch. So I ended up going to a completely different shopping center. I couldn't believe my eyes. I not only found one dress but three. I picked the one that fit me the best and went to lunch.

At the retreat we gave in spring of 2005, I discussed this whole process and how powerful prayer was, especially intercessory prayers. After I told this story, a woman about my size said she was experiencing the same problem. She stated that her daughter was getting married in two weeks and she needed a dress. She not only needed a dress but didn't have the money to buy it. I offered to lend her my dress. She was grateful and the dress fit her perfectly.

This was not a coincidence because there is no such thing. This was God working His plan. I love being an instrument of His Will.

— Anne Pauly

nineteen

Midnight Miracle

For I know the plans that I have for you,
declares the Lord, plans for welfare and not for
calamity to give you a future and a hope.

— Jeremiah 29:11

O NE EVENING IN THE spring of 1998, my sixteen-year-old son left home around 6 p.m. to spend the night at his friend's house. Around midnight, I received a phone call from the police department. They said that my son had been arrested. They asked if I would come to pick him up. The police found him lying face down in the middle of a busy street. He was so drunk he did not know where he was, or how he had gotten there. The policeman said it was a miracle he wasn't killed because that evening it was very dark, it had been raining, and he had dark-colored clothing on. The speed limit on that road was 45 mph. It was difficult to see him lying on the road! It truly was a miracle he was not run over by a car that night!

twenty

Two Wishes

Say to God, "How awesome are Your works!"
— Psalms 66:3

O N FEBRUARY 3, 2005, my mother-in-law's physical therapist told her
a story about her mother. This story took place several years ago in
Poland. The therapist has given her permission to share her story. The
names have been changed.

My mother, Sophie, was sick for a long time. She suffered for so many months
from different problems. She told me that she wished for an easy death. She hoped
for a death by heart attack.

A short time later, aunt Elizabeth went to visit my mother. My mother told her,
that at her funeral, she wished to wear a dress with pearls along the neckline.

Several days later she died. Her death came quickly and with little suffering,
just as she desired. I had the responsibility of making all the funeral arrangements.
When most of the arrangements were made, I asked the funeral director if he had
any dresses I could buy for her funeral.

He took me to a room. After looking at many dresses, I chose a pale beige dress
with pearls around the neckline and also at the waist.

During the wake, aunt Elizabeth knelt by the casket. That is when she noticed the dress my mother was wearing.

Then my aunt asked me, "When did Sophie describe the dress she wanted to be buried in?"

I replied, "Mom never told me what dress she wanted to wear." My mother received the second wish she described to my aunt.

twenty-one

The Fire

Heaven and earth will pass away,
but My words will not pass away.
— Matthew 24:35

WHEN I WAS GROWING up my grandmother always told me, "The Bible never burns. The words of the Bible will never burn." I never really thought much about this until I was older.

In 1987, when I was a single girl, I purchased a mobile home. I found a lovely mobile home park with great neighbors. I always spoke to my neighbors, and they were very pleasant to me.

After I moved in, disturbing things began to happen to me. First, someone put sugar in my gas tank. Next, I began to get prank phone calls. (Someone would call and then hang up.)

About one week later, while my parents were out for dinner, my mom felt that there was something wrong. Before they even got their food she said, "Something is wrong at Renee's house." She had a bad feeling, so they left without finishing their dinner.

When they arrived at my residence, they immediately could see that my mobile home was on fire. One of my neighbors noticed the fire and called the fire department before my parents arrived. I was still at work when I got the news about the fire.

When I got home, I could see that I had lost everything I owned. I couldn't live in the mobile home, and I didn't have any insurance on my home or belongings. The smoke damaged all of my possessions. When the fire was out, I went inside to see if there was anything that could be saved. All I had were the clothes on my back and my car. I looked through drawers and found one thing that was salvageable. It was the Bible my grandmother had given me. It was singed all around the outside, but the words of the Bible were not burned. That is when I remembered what my grandmother said, "The Bible will never burn." **It was true!**

To view photos of the trailer home and Bible go to:

www.touchedbythegraceofGod.com

www.facebook.com (Enter *Touched by the Grace of God* in the search window.)

twenty-two

Going to Heaven

"Truly, truly I say to you, he who hears My word,
and believes Him who sent Me, has eternal life,
and does not come into judgment, but has passed
out of death into life."

— John 5:24

I HAVE BEEN A NURSE for sixteen years, and I have worked in a nursing home for over twenty years. About one year after I became a nurse, I was witness to God's generosity and open arms.

I took care of a patient, Angie, who was terminally ill with cancer. The cancer had spread all over her body and was visible on her neck, where it was ready to penetrate her carotid artery. When that happened, she would quickly bleed to death and her suffering would be over. She was in a tremendous amount of pain and taking several powerful pain medications, but the medications never took all the pain away.

Angie's family told us when she was admitted that she was an atheist. She had never believed in God or gone to church, and they felt she would not want any clergy called in the event of her death.

After Angie had been with us about one month, she started to seep blood from her neck. There was not a great deal of blood at any one time, but it was constant. My co-workers and I felt she could go at any time. We waited and kept vigil over her for three days. Her skin was so pale it was almost pure white from loss of blood, but still she continued to hang on.

On the morning of the fourth day, when I arrived for work, Angie was still there. She was still hanging on. I talked with two other nurses, who felt she was scared to die. She had spent her whole life denouncing God, and now she was facing her moment of truth. She was scared. They both agreed. We discussed calling our in-house clergy to say a prayer over her but didn't want to go against the wishes of the family. So, when I was done with my morning med pass, about 9 a.m., I went to her bedside and said to her, "Don't be afraid to let go. God will take care of you when you leave here." I was called out of her room to attend to another patient. When I returned twenty minutes later, she was gone. I felt very confident she had gone straight to heaven and that I had helped somehow, in some way.

The next morning, I talked with the same two nurses and confessed to them what I had told Angie the day before, just twenty minutes before she died. They were watching me with wide eyes and mouths open. Then they both said, "We told her the same thing!" One of the nurses worked the night shift and talked to Angie before she left; the other one talked with her about an hour before I did.

Now when I think of Angie, all these years later, I look back on her death with a sense of peace. The memory of Angie will be with me throughout my nursing career.

— Holly Restemayer

• twenty-three •

The Miracle of God's Provision

*Do not worry then, saying, "What will we eat?" or "What will
we drink?" or "What will we wear for clothing?" For the Gentiles
eagerly seek all these things; for your heavenly Father knows that
you need all these things. But seek first His kingdom and His
righteousness, and all these things will be added to you.*

*So do not worry about tomorrow; for tomorrow will care for itself.
each day has enough trouble of its own.*

— Matthew 6:31-34

I WAS LAID OFF in October 2003. The unemployment rate was high, although not quite as high as this first month of 2009. Many people were out of work, attending job fairs for positions many pay grades below that of the positions they'd previously held. I was no exception.

At first I was optimistic, believing that, after the holidays, something would come along. I was collecting unemployment. Ironically, I was getting interviews every single week and getting to the second-round phase. Unfortunately, due to the economy, I was just not receiving job offers. Weeks turned into months and still I had no offer. There were just so many of us who were unemployed.

During this time I learned to truly become dependent on God. There were times that we didn't have money to pay for groceries, the mortgage, or utilities.

As a Christian, I knew God would provide, but I'd never had to depend on Him, or others, so much before. My in-laws were buying our groceries each week. The staff at our children's school made sure we had the necessities for winter and Christmas. God provided for us that entire long year, a little at a time, just enough, moment by moment. God opened up a lot of doors for us through people. We began to depend on people through Him, and His great grace provided for us.

One provision in particular stands out. It was spring 2004; I had been laid off for about six months. President Bush had extended unemployment benefits to one year. We were thankful for that but, after balancing the books one afternoon, I realized that we really were down to our last dollar. We had bills to pay—many more bills than we had dollars.

I was completely devastated. I wanted to provide for my wife and my children, but I couldn't do more than I was doing. My wife was now working full time. I wanted to work so badly, but no doors had opened for me. With tears in my eyes, I told my wife the news. We held each other and wept together. We both felt completely helpless, but somehow God gave us the strength to cling to His Word and His promise to never leave us.

As my wife brushed the tears off my cheeks, she said to me, "Don't worry, honey. For all we know, a check could be in the mail." Of course, she didn't really know how this could be because she wasn't going to be paid for another two weeks. About thirty minutes later, my wife checked our mail. In an envelope addressed to both of us was a $500 check from our church's benevolent fund. Attached to the check was a Post-It note which read, "We love you guys."

We were speechless! Prayer was, of course, an important part of our lives, but we had never before experienced a need for lifted-up prayers and then received an answer to those very prayers less than an hour later. Did we doubt that God could provide for us? No. Did we expect for Him to do so in such a dramatic, timely manner? Definitely not! That experience reinforced our belief that God is involved in our daily lives, that He loves us, and that He'll never leave us. We came to the realization that we may not understand why we are asked to go through particular trials or struggles. However, we knew without a doubt that we would never go through them alone.

My unemployment lasted another six months. There were many little miracles that sustained us along the way. Several more checks were sent to us by caring friends and family (some anonymously). Just one week before my unemployment benefits ran out, the Lord provided for us when I received a job in the warehouse of the company that employs my wife! We have had struggles since that time, but at no other point in our lives have we learned so much about God's love and His faithfulness. He truly is Jehovah Jireh: our God, our Provider.

twenty-four

Bright Light

Every good thing given and every perfect
gift is from above, coming down from the
Father of lights, with whom there is no
variation or shifting shadow.

— James 1:17

I AM TELLING THIS story for my eighty-eight-year-old mother. My mother has been a devoted daughter of the Blessed Virgin. She has prayed to Mary as long as I can remember and mentioned many prayers answered. She prays the rosary daily, and everyone in our family asks her to pray for their intentions. We jokingly say she has a 1-800 number to God.

About ten years ago, my mother was in from Arizona and stayed with me in Arlington Heights, Illinois. I had previously purchased a clear Lucite Madonna from a religious store called "Angel Kisses." I showed my mother the Madonna, and she decided that she had to have one. We went to Angel Kisses and purchased the beautiful Madonna with a pink rosary around her neck.

My mother put the Madonna on the dresser in the room she was sleeping in that night. She woke up in the middle of the night and noticed that the Madonna was glowing. There were no lights on; the glow was coming from the Madonna.

My mother was awestruck. She felt that Mary had made herself known to her. My mother talks about this experience frequently, and it still gives me goosebumps.

— *Phyllis Greco*

twenty-five

Bobby's Surprise

"But you, when you pray, go into your room, close your door and
pray to your Father who is in secret, and your Father who sees
what is done in secret will reward you."

— Matthew 6:6

THIS NEXT STORY IS recounted in an e-mail from a patient who became a friend of mine. We found out that we were on the same spiritual level and eventually became good friends. A few years ago, Bobby and I took a trip to Angel Kisses. She ordered a Queen of the Baby Rosary statue there and had it mailed to her home.

Bobby was suffering from cancer in the last years of her life. She was not well when we took the trip to Angel Kisses. Bobby was heavily medicated and was in considerable pain. She understood that, even though she prayed the rosary often, and suffered with cancer for many years, she must accept God's will.

She told me over and over that I should write a journal about my many experiences. I was not interested in writing in diaries, but I decided to take her advice. So I made notes on calendars about miracles, dreams, and visions. Not all of the dreams or visions are mentioned in this book—only the more significant stories. Then, at the end of the year, I would review the notes and elaborate on the stories for my records.

Bobby is now in heaven. Her husband has given me permission to share her story. We both know that this is what Bobby would have wanted.

2/20/03 10:51:59 PM Central Standard Time

Hi Heidi,

Funny I should hear from you tonight, I was going to send you something interesting that happened to me. I wish I had my act together, and had sent it to you sooner, since I will be in your office tomorrow to finish the work on my tooth. Darn, but that is the way my life goes. It takes me 10 times longer to do something. I am still grateful, after all, that I am still here, and trying to get some things in order, and settled before I have to leave. The way the world is going, I think actually I am the lucky one after all.

Now, to add to your list of interesting things, I have this to tell you. I did not display my statue of the Virgin Mary right away when I got it. I just had mixed feelings, and as usual with me and the medicines I am on, time flies, and before I know it weeks have gone by. Anyway, I put it up about a month ago . . . I think. Since I spend so much time by the computer, I put it in that room, sort of behind me on an angle so that I can easily see it. About a week ago I was saying the rosary by the computer. (Actually I play solitaire while I am praying to keep me centered on what I am doing.) I have a habit of rubbing the beads as I am praying. I was at the second large bead, the one before you start the first decade and of course I was rubbing the icon as I was praying.

All at once, I felt liquid on it. Sort of oily liquid and a lot of it, all of my fingers were not damp, but wet, very wet. There was a fragrance to it. It cleared up my nasal passages immediately. It had a very clean smell to it; not heavy, or sweet. Just a very clean smell and then it suddenly dried up. I was praying on the rosary that I had purchased when I was with you that day. I feel it was a sign to tell me not to worry, that the angels and saints are at my side, and hearing my petitions that I am praying for. I can not tell you how happy I am with that sign that they are with me.

What ever you do, don't worry, just have faith and say the rosary big time now.

Take care.

God Bless.

Bobby

Bobby died on September 28, 2003. Her family was by her side. I am confident that she felt she was surrounded by angels.

A short time later I received a thank you note from her husband and daughters. They thanked me for the Mass intentions I had requested for Bobby at St. Edna Parish and the Mundelein Seminary. That same evening while I was saying my evening prayers I heard Bobby's voice. She said, "Thank you, Heidi."

— the late Bobby Larson

twenty-six

Tithing Miracle

*Instruct those who are rich in this present world not to be conceited
or to fix their hope on uncertainty of riches, but on God, who richly
supplies us with all things to enjoy. Instruct them to do good, to be
rich in good works, to be generous and ready to share, storing up for
themselves the treasure of a good foundation for the future, so that
they may take hold of that which is life indeed.*

— 1 Timothy 6:17-19

IN 1997, MY SISTER Heidi sent a Queen of the Baby Rosary statue to my home. My mother and my daughters were present when I opened the box. We all smelled flowers when the box was opened. We did not know a few weeks earlier, when my sister was showing the statue to one of her patients at the dental office, that her patient smelled a very strong scent of roses. Heidi told me she learned this indicates the presence of the Blessed Mother Mary.

I placed the statue on a recessed shelf in the living room of our home. For some unknown reason the statue kept changing directions and tipping over. Mary preferred to face the front door of our home. Then I decided to place the statue on an angle to face the front door instead of facing forward on the shelf, and the statue stopped tipping over.

A short time later I enrolled in a tithing class at church. We received instructions on how to make the proper tithing decisions to thank our Lord for all that He has done.

I pay our bills at a desk in our living room. Gradually, during the time I was enrolled in the tithing class, our Queen of the Baby Rosary statue began to turn to face my desk, which was in the opposite direction of the front door. I knew that Mary was guiding my tithing. I felt this was my tithing miracle.

twenty-seven

The Dream

Consider it all joy, my brethren, when you
encounter various trials, knowing that the
testing of your faith produces endurance.

— James 1:2-3

ABOUT NINE YEARS AGO, I was a real worrier. At this time I was not tracking with God. Little did I know that He was encouraging me to grow closer to Him!

There were two TV celebrities who died over a brief period of time. One man was a movie critic who died from a brain tumor. The other was a newsman, who also died as a result of a brain tumor. Coincidentally, at the time these deaths occurred, there were reports of a possible link between cell phone use and brain tumors.

One night I had a dream that I had something on my brain. When I woke up, all I could remember from my dream was that I had water on my brain.

I went to see my doctor and asked him if I could have a CAT scan for my peace of mind. He said he thought I was perfectly fine, but he'd write an order for me to get one. I didn't have any symptoms that suggested something was wrong. I just needed to do this. I also wanted my husband, Jim, to go and get checked because he used his cell phone quite a bit.

Jim and I went for the scans together. When my doctor got our test results back, he was in shock. He called and said Jim was fine but that I had a tumor on my brain. He said the tumor was on my brain stem, and that was the worst place because the brain stem is what sends messages to every part of your body. It really hit home for him because his mother had died from a brain tumor.

I thought to myself that here I am with two small children, and I am going to die. I was thinking also that I'm not going to be around to see them grow up. The doctor said this kind of tumor just keeps growing. I could go deaf or maybe even become paralyzed. The worst part was waking up with the sun shining, thinking it's going to be a beautiful day. Then you remember that you have a tumor, and you are wondering just how limited your days are going to be. Every day you are constantly thinking about that.

My doctor referred me to a surgeon friend of his in Chicago. The surgeon told me the tumor was a benign meningioma. That meant it was not cancer. He said it was a slow-growing tumor but that it still would continue to grow and that the symptoms would be bad. He also said that he could do surgery, but the surgery would be very risky because the tumor was on the brain stem. He advised me to wait five or six years, not just because the tumor would grow slowly, but also because I had small children. Then when I became symptomatic, we would schedule surgery. Being the worrier that I was, that was not the news I needed to hear. The surgeon seemed so very uncaring. I left there crying and extremely upset.

Each morning I would go down to the basement bathroom, where no one would see me, and I cried. I reached out to God and asked Him for help.

Jim started doing some research. One evening, as he was changing channels on the television, he caught the last few minutes of 20/20. The discussion focused on the CyberKnife, which is a robotic radiosurgery system for targeting tumors. Tumors are pinpointed using computerized images before radiation, and the radiation is then delivered to the exact location. Ideally, the tumors will shrink or disappear and not return.

You had to be a candidate to have the procedure done, and I was definitely a candidate. Now I know that it was God who sent Jim the message on the television that night. I called the number Jim had written down and left a message. They got back to me right away. I sent them my brain scans. The doctors wanted me to come to San Francisco to meet with them at Stanford University. They said I should have this procedure done while the tumor was still small. In the meantime, I had been reading all the books I could get my hands on about God. I just wanted to know more about Him.

Jim and I scheduled the procedure for a month later. When we left that day and walked outside, there was the most beautiful double rainbow! That was the first double rainbow I had ever seen. At that moment I knew that I was going to be fine.

Jim and I flew to Stanford to have the procedure done. It was a two-day process, although I was only there an hour each day. Dr. Chang and his team were the kindest people I have ever met. I know God led us to them!

We flew home from Stanford on Thanksgiving Day, and it was the Thanksgiving of my life. I had my life back when I was informed that the procedure was a **success**!

This was the point in my life when I realized God shows up in the most magnificent way! He reached into my soul, saved me from a living hell, and lit a fire in my heart, which produced a love for Him that continues to grow and is more intense than a blazing fire! My life was changed by Him. I love Him more than my own life now. If anyone still questions whether God exists, seek God while He can still be found!

—*Jolene Pasta*

Visions

twenty-eight

My Childhood Vision

*Heal me, oh Lord, and I will be healed; save me
and I will be saved, for You are my praise.*

— Jeremiah 17:14

S INCE I WAS A young child, I have always felt a strong devotion to our Blessed Mother Mary. My birthday is August 22, which is the feast day of the Queenship of Mary.

One fall when I was five years old (I was the youngest child), my sisters and I all came down with horrible swollen glands. I was having a difficult time recovering. So my mother called the doctor to have him come to our home and check on my condition. On that day he lanced my throat. I was extremely ill, and for several days I lay in bed.

I distinctly remember, one evening after my mother put me to bed, seeing three monks around my bed. I felt afraid and remembered that my sisters told me to make the sign of the cross whenever I was scared. Somehow, as weak as I was, I raised my hand and made the sign of the cross. The monks were talking among themselves. I heard them say, "Not yet." Then they disappeared.

I knew that day when I was so ill that I had experienced a vision. I was about fifteen years old when, for the first time, I mentioned this vision to my sisters. None of my sisters saw the monks.

As I grew up, I continued to feel a devotion to Mary. Coincidentally, I was baptized on the feast day of St. Catherine Laboure. November 27, 1830, is the date Mary presented the Miraculous Medal to St. Catherine Laboure.

twenty-nine

Evening Vision

Just as we have borne the image of the earthy,
we will also bear the image of the heavenly.

— 1 Corinthians 15:49

M Y STORY IS A simple one. I awoke suddenly one night during the last week of December in 1978. I was very uncomfortable, because of my oversized abdomen, during my sixth month of pregnancy. I decided to sit on the side of my bed to adjust my nightgown and blankets.

I looked at the door to our bedroom. There I saw a vision of my father. He smiled and looked in and then walked to the boys' room. He then proceeded to do the same thing by the nursery, where my little daughter slept. Finally, he came back, looked at me, nodded his head and smiled. The vision began to disappear as if it were a prism of shattering glass.

A week later my dad passed away of a massive heart attack. I think God was giving me a message that even today I can't forget. His message to me is that, no matter what struggles or conflicts I must face, my primary concern should be to guide and protect my children, who God has entrusted to my care.

thirty

The Night I'll Never Forget

"Have I not commanded you? Be strong and
courageous! Do not tremble or be dismayed, for
the Lord your God is with you wherever you go."
— Joshua 1:9

FOR MORE THAN TEN years I've walked and jogged about six miles every night around Lake Arlington. Lake Arlington is a man-made lake, which is about two miles in circumference, and is located on the northeast side of Arlington Heights, Illinois. I run two miles to the lake. I feel this place is like "heaven." As I exercise, I pray. I treasure the night. Each evening I love to greet the moon and the stars above me. I cannot explain the beauty of these evenings. I'm almost ashamed to say I'm not terrified to get up and walk in the middle of the night.

August 15, 2002, was like any other night at the end of August. I performed my nightly jogging toward Lake Arlington. It was a very beautiful, peaceful night. There were no people at the lake and no noise coming from any cars on busy Windsor Drive.

Occasionally, I would see a police car drive through the parking lot. The police officers all knew me and probably were saying, "There is that crazy woman walking in the middle of the night!"

When I am walking I know that I am not really alone. I believe that God is cheering me on whenever I am running.

I take a deep breath and thank God for what He has done for me the previous day. I pray for my husband, myself, my daughter, her husband, and their children. Then I pray, "Okay Lord, show up big time. I do need You very much today, Jesus." Sometimes, I feel I'm always begging God for something. Often my prayers are for friends or neighbors who are in despair and in need of various kinds of help. I do know God's goal is to rescue us from evil. There is no monkey wrench in God's plan. Each day I plead with God for the grace to be faithful to Him. I've prayed, "Dear God, where there is darkness please understand I need You to end my fear." That provides my daily encouragement.

But this night on the other side of the lake, I saw a dark van with the taillights on. I have never seen a car parked, in that area, on the bicycle path. At first, I thought maybe the van would move to the street. As I walked a little closer to the curve of the lake, I became a little suspicious. I thought, "Why is that van still here? Could I be attacked? I'm a very healthy woman, and I can run, but what if there are several of them?" I wanted to finish my lap around Lake Arlington, and then I decided, "No, I shouldn't be frightened. I have God next to me, to be my custodian angel. I will be okay."

At the very moment I decided that I should not go another step closer to the van, God showed me a symbol. I was stopped like a stumbling block by a most beautifully tinted multicolored cloud. There is no doubt in my mind that this was a symbol of God's grace holding me back, so I would not go any closer to that van. I decided to turn around. God with His enduring love was taking care of me.

At that moment God completely led me to safety. The cloud of light completely covered me. I was filled with heavenly peace. In my disbelief of what had just happened, I started to weep. I turned around and walked home. When I got home, I thanked God on my knees for taking care of me, and I also realized that that day was the holy day of the Assumption of the Blessed Virgin Mary.

I'm certain God still has work for me to do, because for some reason He protected me that evening. I also know He saved me for a purpose, which only increases my determination to do all I can do for Him while I am alive. Life is a gift—one I'll use to bring Him glory.

Lake Arlington and
My Truest Friend: God

Deep in the silence of the lake
was where I'd go to be, that I might
hear in nature's stillness
God's voice speaking to me.
His voice, it echoes through the trees
when the wind caresses their limbs
like angels softly whispering,
"Please open wide your door,
and you will find the love and peace
you've never known before."
Each time that I think of You,
it causes me to smile.
You have done so much for me.
You make my life worthwhile.
You've been on hand when came my way
a test, or trial, or scare.
Things within myself I thought unfit
and so denied, but sharing frees me to admit.
So many things I have seen here
Your very chief concern:
and as the pathway of this life
makes here and there a turn,
You've been at every road with me,
a helping hand to lend.
That's why I'll always treasure You,
my God, my truest Friend.

SECTION FOUR

Out of Body Experiences

thirty-one

A Physician's Faith

The Lord is my shepherd, I shall not want. He makes me lie down in green pastures; He leads me beside quiet waters. He restores my soul; He guides me in the paths of righteousness for His name's sake. Even though I walk through the valley of the shadow of death, I fear no evil, for You are with me; Your rod and Your staff, they comfort me. You prepare a table before me in the presence of my enemies; You have anointed my head with oil; my cup overflows. Surely goodness and loving kindness will follow me all the days of my life, and I will dwell in the house of the Lord forever.

— Psalms 23:1-6

DURING MY YEARS AS a physician I experienced moments that reinforced my belief in God. I think I have to say that if the pursuit of a premedical career had been one of the things that caused me to stray from my spiritual journey, it was the practice of medicine that brought me back. As an M.D., I've seen a lot of people suffer. Some of the most miraculous healings I've seen, however, came not from me or anything I did. I think they came from love or the power of love. It was this interconnection between the patient and the people around him, who love him (or her), that made all the difference between recovering or not. Even in the cases of patients who were dying, or lying on their death beds, I sometimes would notice something paradoxical and yet quite wonderful. There seemed to come a point when the patient would stop struggling and arrive at a stage of acceptance. It was like, all of a sudden, these entire outer layers would peel off, and underneath these layers emerged this clear picture of a beautiful person who had found peace and serenity, as well as acceptance. There are so many mysteries in this world. As an M.D., I always wondered why there seemed to be so much unnecessary and meaningless suffering in the world. Why do bad things seem to happen to good people? Well, I don't pretend to have the answers, but I do have an observation to make after I experienced my own pain and suffering. It was the pain that caused me to change. It prompted me to work and learn and then to move on to a new and higher level of understanding; but before I could do that, I had to face the pain. You know, I don't think we're going to have it all together, where there's no work, no frustration, or any pain. That's not reality. Living is work and a four-letter word we call pain. It's not negative. It's what led me back to God. It brought me back to my Christian faith.

I really like the words of noted author Kierkegaard. He says, "Life can only be understood backwards, but it must be lived forward." I have to look backwards when I try to understand three different experiences that happened to me at different times in my life. These experiences were actually more like signposts to me because they helped guide me back to my own Christianity. I want you to know that I have shared these experiences with less than a handful of people in all these years, and there were a number of reasons for this. I have to confess that one of the reasons I wasn't going to share these experiences is that these experiences will sound like something coming out of the *Twilight Zone*. Yet these things happened and they most certainly were important. So after giving it a lot of thought, I decided that I really ought not to leave this out.

The first experience happened actually about twenty years ago. It was late at night. I was at the hospital in the coronary care unit. I had just finished seeing and examining a middle-aged gentleman who was being admitted at the time with the diagnosis of unstable angina. I was just finishing up writing in his chart when suddenly the alarm went off from the cardiac monitor, and it was coming from this man's room.

There were only two nurses on duty that evening. (And maybe an aide: I don't remember.) We all jumped up and ran into his room. I could see from the monitor that he was in ventricular fibrillation (that is, his heart was fluttering, but not pumping any blood).

One of the nurses immediately called a "Code Blue," which is actually a medical team trained to deal with these kinds of emergencies. Fortunately, we didn't have to wait for them. A cardiac defibrillator was nearby, and one of the nurses quickly wheeled it in. I immediately shocked his heart. Nothing happened, so I shocked him a few more times, and we had to do some CPR. This time it worked, and a normal looking heartbeat appeared on the monitor.

In a matter of seconds his color had returned, and his blood pressure had come up, and he said to me in a real urgent, excited kind of voice, "Don't worry about me, doc; I'm okay, but there's a guy in the next room in trouble. I think he's having a heart attack." No sooner had he said that when the alarm from the monitor went off again, and this time it was coming from the man in the next room, exactly as my patient had said. At that point the crew from Code Blue had arrived in our room. Now we suddenly realized we were needed in that other room, so we all had to turn around and rush into the other room.

When this was all over, I returned to my patient's room wanting to know from him what had happened. I sat and listened in utter amazement as he told me about the sensation he had of floating over the bed, and how he was able to look down and see and hear everything that was going on; but he also seemed to know what was happening to the man in the other room. He told me that, after I shocked his heart, he felt himself being drawn back into his body. He also said that he "saw" the man in the next room, but I couldn't help being struck by the fact that there happened to be a wall there between him and the man in the next room. He also said he felt compelled to tell me what was happening in the next room.

The two nurses that witnessed this were equally dumbfounded, and I might add that so was the patient. In fact, he started to get so excited that we started to worry about his heart and needed to calm him down. One of the nurses, who was religious, said to me that she thought it was a miracle from God. I was thinking the same thing, too, as I drove home that evening.

I have to say that this all happened at a time in my life when I was having serious problems in my first marriage. My wife had moved out with my son to an apartment. I was alone, depressed, and feeling like a failure; but after having had that experience I seemed to feel much better. My depression seemed to lift, and my problems didn't feel so major anymore. Over the course of the next several weeks, I pondered over the meaning of what I had witnessed. We had estimated that my patient was clinically dead for at least four minutes and maybe as long as five minutes. Finally, I had to come to the conclusion that it had to be true after all: **life really doesn't end with death**. How else could I explain what I had witnessed that night?

A number of years passed, it was 1980, and I had recently married my second wife. Around that time my father, who never drank, had been diagnosed as having cancer of the liver. We watched him over a period of months become progressively weaker to the point that he was unable to get out of bed. His abdomen had filled with fluid, and his skin and eyes turned yellow from jaundice.

We knew the end was in sight. At the time, it was my mother's wish that my dad should die in his own home with dignity, instead of in some hospital bed. As was the custom in our family, it was our wish to be at the bedside when his time came. Our immediate family group consisted of my brother and his wife, my aunt, my second wife, me, and of course my mom.

We knew the time had come because my father lapsed into a coma and began hemorrhaging from his GI tract. His blood pressure had dropped to a very low reading. For almost forty-eight hours continuously, his pulse and respirations increased while his coma deepened.

So, we all started saying the rosary and later reading passages from the Bible. The hours went by. We all became exhausted. We had kept a constant vigil, non-stop for almost forty-eight hours. We all started taking turns, trying to sleep in shifts. I had just started to lie down in one of the bedrooms when all of a sudden

I heard my wife come running to the bedroom yelling at the top of her lungs: "John, John, hurry, hurry; something's happening to your father; hurry, I think he's waking up."

I leaped out of bed and ran to his bedroom. All of us had gathered in a semicircle around his bed. It was **true**; not only had he awakened, but he was completely awake. That was the first miracle because medically I was totally at a loss to explain how he had awakened from such a deep coma. The second miracle all of us saw was that the yellow color in his eyes from the jaundice was gone. His eyes looked clear. He said nothing, but his eyes seemed to focus sharply on each one of us, until finally his eyes settled on my mother for the longest time. If his eyes could talk, I knew he was telling her how much he loved her for the last time. Just at that moment his eyes rolled upward and he died. Now, the third miracle: my wife (of all people), my brother and sister-in-law, and my mother, all claimed they saw a transparent, colorless mist rise up out of his body at the moment his eyes rolled up. I don't know why, but I never saw it.

Now I would like to point out one thing from the last miracle here: if there was anyone I knew that was agnostic, it had to be my last wife. Actually she was practically an atheist. I always thought that, to listen to her talk. But that night she came up to me and said that she would never again doubt the existence of God after what she had seen happen that night. That was a miracle, for her. She had been, like all of us, deeply moved by this spiritual experience. My father's death had turned out to be a joyful and deeply spiritual experience. That happened more than thirty years ago, but in my mind it seems like it was just yesterday.

Lastly, I'd like to briefly tell you about my own personal spiritual experience. It's nowhere as astonishing as my dad's. This happened only about fourteen years ago. At that time I was a one and a half pack a day cigarette smoker. Even though I had tried to quit, I was never successful. One day while showering, I noticed a lump on the left side of my neck. It was just above my clavicle, but it felt unusually hard. Over the course of the next few weeks, the lump increased markedly in size. Now I was feeling more than one mass. Talk about denial. I just couldn't get myself to accept the idea that something potentially terrible might be happening in my body.

Finally, I just couldn't ignore it any longer. My worst fear surfaced because I knew as a medical doctor that the first thing a doctor would think of would be cancer of the lung, based on finding a hard mass in this location just above the clavicle in a person who smoked like I did and had such a strong positive family history of cancer. I also knew, as an M.D., that if this turned out to be cancer of the lung, my prognosis was hopeless because it had already spread outside the chest cavity. This meant that it was now inoperable and metastatic (meaning it had spread) in which case, even with treatment, I was likely to be dead in six months.

Finally, I got up the courage and made an appointment to see one of my friends, Dr. Jackson, who is a lung specialist. As he examined my neck, I could see the worried expression on his face. Finally he strained to control his voice. He told me the mass felt suspicious. He got on the phone and called a surgeon, Dr. Burke, another friend of mine. After examining my neck, Dr. Burke told me the same thing Dr. Jackson had said. He then proceeded to schedule me for a biopsy of the neck mass the following day.

I cancelled my office hours for the next day. As I drove home my entire body felt numb. I couldn't believe this was happening to me. My mind was racing as I tried to sort out for myself what I should do for the short time I had left. I knew one thing: I wasn't going to take any radiation therapy or chemotherapy.

I thought of closing my office and spending the rest of my time with my family and friends. I can't begin to describe all the emotions I felt. My immediate family members were all in New York visiting my nephew, who was celebrating the birth of his new daughter. I decided not to call them and spoil their trip. They would find out soon enough, I thought.

That night as I lay in bed, I really began to feel sorry for myself. So many things that I had hoped would happen in my life just never happened. I had just recently been through my second divorce. I was really feeling like some kind of failure, and now this was happening to me. I remember lying in bed that night feeling emotionally and physically exhausted. I couldn't help feeling that God must have thought I was unimportant and insignificant and that my life never counted and I never counted. I remember crying to myself in bed that night, as I fell asleep exhausted.

Now, I would like to say that I never had dreamt of Him, nor have I ever dreamt of Him since, but that night I had a dream; and in this dream Christ came to me. In the dream there was a table with two chairs. We sat down. On the table was what seemed to be a couple of beans and a cup. Jesus picked up the two beans and placed them in the cup. He shook the cup and out came a pair of dice. The number seven came up. Just at that moment I woke up and it was morning.

I suddenly realized in my heart of hearts that I was going to be okay. Not only had Jesus come to me in my dream to tell me that I would be okay but that, by coming to me in my dream, He showed me that I did count after all. After that, my entire mood changed 180 degrees. I became as happy as a lark. I remember smiling ear to ear as I walked into that surgical room to have my biopsy done that morning. I remember Dr. Burke and his nurse staring at me like I was crazy. It turned out to be a rather rare, but benign, tumor. I'd also like to say that I've never picked up another cigarette since, and that happened over five years ago.

For me this had been truly a gift of grace, a miracle bringing me face to face with myself, my God, and my Christianity. Today I'm a Christian. I celebrate being a Christian because it is more than just a belief system or a set of rules. It's a way of living and thinking. It's a constant reminder to us that Christ came down to earth and died for us, so that we would no longer be separated from God. Christ spoke to His Apostles about the Kingdom of Heaven being within us. I think we all have the Divine Spark within us, but I think we have to find it, each in our own way and each in our own time. I believe that most of us, sooner or later, will come to realize that the emptiness or void we often sense in our lives can ultimately be traced back to our separation from God. But the joy of our Christian awareness is that, when Christ died for us, the door of separation opened. Our spiritual journey, therefore, is a journey that will ultimately take us to our final destination: back to where our true home is: back to God.

thirty-two

Childbirth Complications

Therefore, being always of good courage, and knowing that while
we are at home in the body we are absent from the Lord-for we
walk by faith, not by sight-we are of good courage, I say, and prefer
rather to be absent from the body and to be at home with the Lord.

— 2 Corinthians 5:6-8

O N NOVEMBER 17, 1965, at 2 a.m., I delivered my son Joe. Around 3 a.m., I began bleeding heavily while I was in the delivery/recovery room. One LPN on duty that morning refused my requests to reach my obstetrician. She stated that I was just worrying too much and that my bleeding was normal. I was also an RN and tried to convey to her that something was definitely wrong.

So, I requested a phone to call my husband, Ted. I told him to get my OB over immediately, as I was in danger. Both Ted and my OB were there within fifteen minutes. They got me ready to go into surgery. Yes, I was really losing blood quickly.

I experienced a sense of floating above the bed. I could see Ted and the doctor. I felt sad that I would be leaving my new baby and Ted. There was also a sense of peace.

Behind me, as I was hovering, I saw a tunnel, a walkway, a path, etc. There was a brilliant light at the other end. That was all I saw. I heard nothing. Then I was sewn up for my bleeder, given transfusions, and was fine.

I only shared this information with my husband Ted. For many years I thought it was a dream or a hallucination due to blood loss. Years later, I understood what had happened to me. After reading Elizabeth Kubler-Ross, and hearing her speak at Harper College in Palatine, Illinois, I realized that this was normal with near-death experiences. It still is not a story I share with many people.

thirty-three

"Please, Just Let Me Stay!"

If Christ is in you, though the body is dead because of sin, yet the spirit is alive because of righteousness. But if the Spirit of Him who raised Jesus from the dead dwells in you, He who raised Christ Jesus from the dead will also give life to your mortal bodies through His Spirit who dwells in you.

— Romans 8:10-11

MY HUSBAND, DON, was always so busy working, spending time on the computer, and involved with so many church activities that my sons and I barely spent any time with him, and we felt invisible. We would have dinner together, but then he would go to church meetings. (He joined the Knights of Columbus and became a Grand Knight.) His outside activities were important, but my sons and I missed him. Many times I told him that God wouldn't want him to live this way and that his church activities were great but his family should be in the picture, too.

I will never forget February 5, 2004. That morning Don kissed me goodbye and left for work. I felt incredibly weak and was experiencing hot and cold flashes. I thought I was getting the flu and told my older son, Alex, to take care of his younger brother Kyle. I was too weak to get out of bed and drive Kyle to school. I hoped taking Nyquil would resolve my symptoms and help me sleep. (I found out later from my doctor that, if I did go to sleep, I might not have awakened.)

That afternoon I was supposed to leave my car at the mechanics to have it serviced. Don was going to call me at 4:45 p.m. to find out if he should pick me up and drive me home. (Later that day we were planning to leave for a snowmobiling trip to Wisconsin with our neighbors. Don's snowmobile was ready for the weekend trip, and our family was excited.) When he called me I said, "Don, I can't go anywhere. I can't even get out of bed. Something is wrong; I am really sick."

When Don came home from work, he talked to me in our bedroom before he left for his church meeting. I told him that I was so sick that I didn't take Alex to school. I guess because I was lying in bed he couldn't really tell how sick I was. He went to his church meeting anyway.

When Don came home at 8:30 p.m., he asked whether I was feeling better and I replied that I had never felt as sick as this before in my life. When I stood up to get back into bed, Don said I turned white as a ghost and started to mumble. He caught me just before I hit my head on the vanity. I quit breathing.

When I came to, Don was on the phone telling a 911 operator that I may have suffered a seizure and passed out. At this moment I felt as if I was outside of my body and was dying.

When the paramedics arrived, they brought me downstairs in a special carrier and transferred me to a stretcher in the kitchen. I quit breathing two more times and had more seizures. This is difficult to believe, but all of a sudden I felt like I was on the other side of the kitchen by the sliding doors. I could see firemen, paramedics, policemen, my neighbors, the kids, the dog, and Don in the kitchen.

One paramedic was slapping my hand saying, "Cindy, are you with us? Cindy, are you still with us?"

I couldn't answer him. (They later told me I was not breathing.) I was watching him and thinking, "No, I am not with you." I didn't know where I was. I could feel him hit me again, and when I looked at him I knew I was back in my body. It was the weirdest experience I've ever had. It was very peaceful wherever I was, but I wanted to stay and live.

The paramedic was hitting my hand again and asking me, "Cindy, are you with us?"

I said, "Yes, I am with you." For a few minutes I wasn't and they were frantic.

This was making me extremely nervous. It was peaceful there, and I remember saying to God, "I know You will take me if You want to. I know that I don't really have a say-so in that matter, but I really want to stay because I have little kids. **Please just let me stay!**"

It was snowing like crazy outside. As the paramedics carried me to the ambulance, I wished they would lay me in the snow to cool off before we left for the hospital. It took forever to get to St. Joseph's Hospital, in Elgin, Illinois, because the roads were horrible.

I found out later that while I was in the ambulance my blood pressure was 80/0 and the paramedics put me upside down to help me get a blood pressure. Nothing worked. During this time I had another seizure and quit breathing again. I was on the verge of dying.

Don didn't come to the hospital until he made arrangements for the kids. When he finally came into the room, he looked very scared and left to find a nurse. Shortly after the nurse arrived, she immediately left for additional help because my blood pressure dropped to 80/0 and I had another seizure.

I felt bizarre during those seizures. I told my husband later that I thought I was singing church hymns. Don said, "No, Cindy you weren't singing."

The doctor finally came in and said, "You are too young to be this sick." He wanted to know how I became so dehydrated, and I told him I had no idea.

My second chest X-ray indicated that my lungs were now three quarters full of pneumonia. The doctor told me if I had another seizure he would have to induce a coma. (I was afraid I would never wake up if he did.)

After I suffered another seizure, the doctor did induce a coma. I remember dreaming about having an ice cube. I was so thirsty.

When I came to, I was on life support and had a tube down my throat, a needle in my chest, and a needle in my kidneys. I was also unable to talk or write. The doctors thought I might have been in cardiac arrest or possibly have kidney or heart failure, and I learned I had septic shock when I arrived at the hospital.

I noticed that my parents, who live in North Carolina, were sitting in the room with Don. Don asked me what day it was, and I answered Friday, because I thought

I was taken to the hospital on Thursday. When he told me it was Sunday, I wondered what had happened to the two missing days. Don told me he had been with me the entire time, praying over and over, and that our priest Father Joe had given me last rites. People at church and in the neighborhood were praying for me as well.

When I fell into the coma, the doctors told Don I'd probably be in intensive care for weeks or months, if I survived at all. I found out later that I had the bacterial pneumonia that the puppeteer Jim Henson died from. After my recovery a nurse at the hospital told me that three months earlier a young woman had died of this disease.

After I left the hospital, I had physical therapy to strengthen my muscles and to learn to walk again. I didn't look well, but gradually I became independent again thanks to my husband.

I couldn't go to church for two months because I needed to avoid germs. One Sunday I finally saw Father Joe at church and said, "I am sorry you had to see me like that."

He said, "Like what?" Apparently he was used to seeing very ill patients.

A few months later Don and I saw the nun from the hospital at a church function. When I spoke to her, she looked as if she was talking to the living dead. She was so amazed that it appeared as if nothing had happened to me.

At my two-week checkup my doctor said, "You know, Cindy, there is no medical reason why you are here. It can't be explained medically." I know I am here because of the **grace of God**. It can be explained through God.

This was an incredibly frightening experience for Don. He felt so helpless and prayed constantly at my bedside. Don said he would have traded places with me if he could have! His faith and love helped me during my recovery.

Today I am fine, and I thank God that he let me stay here. To think that one day you are fine and the next day you are literally on your death bed is very frightening. I think there is a lesson to be learned from this. Now, when I get up in the morning, I am just grateful to be alive. I hope this feeling will always stay with me. I know every day is a test. I will never take life for granted again. If you don't have your health, you don't have anything. **It is a miracle that I am here!**

— *Cindy White*

thirty-four

The Tunnel of Light

This is the message we have heard from Him and announce to you, that God is Light, and in Him there is no darkness at all.

— 1 John 1:5

O NE DAY IN 1992, I went for a routine CT scan at Northwest Community Hospital in Arlington Heights, Illinois. I filled out all the paperwork prior to having the scan. I indicated under the allergy section that I was allergic to fish.

The technician insisted that I needed to have the dye inserted into the IV for better contrast. I was very apprehensive because of my past experiences, knowing how medications have produced side effects. As they proceeded, the technician assured me, "I am right here, just call if you need help."

No sooner had the dye been administered when I felt as though I could not breathe, and everything was getting very black. I shouted, "I can't breathe!" Time stood still.

Then I was walking down a very dark tunnel, at the end of which was a spot of light. As I walked, I felt a presence at my side. I didn't see anyone. I just felt as though I was not alone.

The farther I walked into the tunnel, the brighter the light became. The thought came to my mind that I was dying, and my husband was going to be alone when he would get the terrible news. My other thought was of my children, and it broke my heart to have to leave them. At this point, I became very angry, turned, kicked the wall, and said, "This is a heck of a way to die."

As I looked back at the beginning of the tunnel, I was suddenly back in the room where I had been for my CT scan. With the sound of a swish, I felt a pressure on my forehead and chest, and then I was back in my body. When my husband saw me, he was shocked at my appearance, because my eyes were swollen and my face was flushed.

Angels

thirty-five

Peggy Ann

There are also heavenly bodies and earthly
bodies, but the glory of the heavenly is one,
and the glory of the earthly is another.

— 1 Corinthians 15:40

THIS STORY IS ABOUT my precious little daughter Peggy Ann. She was born in 1950, on our fifth wedding anniversary.

Peggy was born with cystic fibrosis. It is an incurable disease. One person in twenty is a carrier. Both parents must be carriers to produce this condition. We had never heard of this disease. The parents' chances are one in four of having a child with this disease.

Peggy Ann was a very religious child. When we would read the Bible together while she took breathing treatments, she would explain a passage to me if I didn't understand it.

At the age of ten, Peggy Ann died from this disease. Just before she died, she experienced a heavenly visit from her guardian angel.

Peggy Ann woke up during the night and saw a figure by her bed. Peggy went to the bathroom, thinking it would go away, but it followed her.

The next morning she told me about it. I said, "Why didn't you wake me up? Were you scared?"

She said, "No," and went back to bed.

A few days later she went to heaven to join her baby brother, who had preceded her in death with the same fatal disease. Some time later, her daddy also joined her in heaven.

I was blessed with a longer life. I enjoy my life with my wonderful son Bill, daughter Sue, and five delightful grandchildren.

Peggy Ann loved stories about miracles. She was always hoping for one. She would also say, "I'll be glad when I can go to heaven; then I won't have to have this disease."

— Betty Borgeson

thirty-six

April 23, 1993

*Do not neglect to show hospitality to
strangers, for by this some have entertained
angels without knowing it.*

— Hebrews 13:2

O N APRIL 23, 1993, our lives changed forever. My husband, Michael, was hurt pulling out old bushes at work. He ruptured a disk in his back that required surgery. Unfortunately, something went wrong during surgery that damaged all the nerves that control your body from the waist down.

Michael said immediately that his lower body was numb, and he could not lift his legs. After months of physical rehab, we were told that the nerves were permanently damaged and that he would always have pain and great difficulty walking.

Michael is a strong man with great faith; he never gave up trying to get physically stronger. He worked daily on walking with less assistance. Over time he was able to get around better, but the pain was increasing, and muscle spasms began to take over his nights. The less sleep he got, the weaker he became, and he fell on difficult times. He always had a positive attitude and never complained. He knew that God was watching over him.

On December 6, 1999, six and a half years after the accident, we received a beautiful floral delivery for our thirtieth wedding anniversary. The deliveryman asked Michael what was wrong with him. So, Mike explained the situation.

The kind gentleman suggested that Mike start taking Omega 3 capsules to help his condition. Mike thanked him for the suggestion and the flowers. Then the deliveryman was off to his next delivery.

Michael had taken many prescription meds for pain and spasms, with no success. We weren't sure about the Omega 3 but felt—what could it hurt? So Mike began taking Omega 3 in December 1999. After several weeks, Mike asked me to buy more because he felt a little relief from the spasms. Over time, we both noticed an improvement in Mike's general well-being.

He was getting more sleep at night and having fewer spasms. In time Mike was able to withdraw from the prescription spasm meds, but remained on the Omega 3.

It has been more than twelve years since our angel flower man came to our door. Michael has made great progress. He walks with one cane, has very few spasms, and is able to enjoy his grandchildren.

God sent us an angel. **Thank you God!**

— *Ginger Mueller*

thirty-seven

Angels in Our Midst

But now faith, hope, love abide these three:
but the greatest of these is love.

— 1 Corinthians 13:13

GOD OFTEN PLACES ANGELS in the most unlikely places. I was never more convinced of that than when my daughter, Kim, faced catastrophic illness at the age of twenty-seven, while living in Spain. I had been back to work for just one week, following my own successful colon cancer surgery in November of 2003, when I received a call from Kim's roommate that put me in frantic, desperate mother mode. I was informed that Kim had collapsed in the apartment that the two young women shared in Barcelona, had aspirated vomit, and was in a coma in critical condition in the ICU. Her roommate urged me to get on the next flight to Barcelona, and I wasn't sure my daughter would still be alive when I arrived.

The eight-hour flight was horrifying . . .I was in constant prayer, with fitful dreams of bringing back her body and awarding a scholarship in her name at the school where I work. I was met at the airport by strangers who would later become very close to me . . .the first of many angels to care for me during the ordeal. Kim's co-workers and friends, many of whom spoke little or no English, welcomed and comforted me, as we rushed to her bedside at the hospital. I nearly fainted at the sight of my daughter hooked up to a respirator, and connected to what seemed like a dozen tubes and beeping monitors.

For one month, Kim remained on life support, suffering from Acute Respiratory Distress Syndrome, pneumonia, a staph infection, and a collapsed lung. She received sedation and a tracheotomy to facilitate ventilation. Just before Christmas, she awoke and we shared a joyous, emotional reunion with my other daughter, Beth, who flew from Los Angeles to be with us. The sight of the two sisters embracing was one I will never forget. Their love was never so apparent as the reality registered that we had almost lost Kim! We thanked God that she was fine neurologically, and that she was able to speak all three of her languages without any damage to her wonderful brain!

As Kim became aware of what had happened to her, we started to put together all of the pieces surrounding her collapse. An avid runner, Kim had become ill at work after a workout and was advised by a clinic at her university that she was dehydrated. She went home and drank lots of water, which ironically was the worst thing she could have done, since she actually had an electrolyte imbalance. All the remaining sodium was washed out of her body and that water "intoxication" triggered her collapse and medical emergency.

Throughout the three difficult months I spent in Barcelona during her recovery and release from the hospital, I encountered many "angels" and found evidence of God at work in everything that happened to us. First, her roommate was about thirty minutes late in leaving their apartment for class that fateful morning. That tardiness allowed her to hear Kim's moans from the upstairs bathroom, which unnoticed, would have meant certain death. The group of "angels" who loved Kim surrounded me like a warm blanket, translating from Spanish and Catalan for me, helping me find my way through a strange city, and giving me the support I needed to get through all this. Their faces at the window of Kim's ICU room, looking at me as I stood at Kim's bedside in sterile garb and a mask, gave me strength and knowledge that God was with us, too, as a family of believers.

Kim's ICU roommate was a teenage boy with Down Syndrome, who was also on a ventilator and in a coma. His wonderful family always inquired about

Kim's progress and offered encouragement when I saw them each day. When the boy passed away, his grieving family kissed him and paid their last visit. His mother and I stood between our children's two beds—her son, dead, and my daughter, clinging to life. We two women held each other and cried together. Neither of us spoke each other's language, but the bond between two mothers is strong and easily understood. The boy's brother continued to come to the hospital for several days, checking on Kim and offering his family's support and prayers for her recovery.

Every Sunday during those first difficult weeks in Barcelona, I attended an English-speaking church. The worshippers there were kind people who always prayed for my daughter and me. A South African woman from the parish was concerned about me, seeing me in my lightweight jacket, which was no longer warm enough for the winter weather. She took the coat off her back and handed it to me, saying, "I have many others and you need this now." This was also the powerful display of God's love through an angel he put in my path.

The people at the school where I work in the Chicago suburbs were very concerned for my family. They collected generous donations for us, which provided funds for my living expenses there, as well as for my other daughter's flight from Los Angeles to Barcelona, so we could all be together for Christmas. My job stayed secure for those three months while I was gone. Prayer warriors at our church back home were petitioning God for Kim's healing, as well as the emotional well-being of our family.

Back in the U.S., my mother, who has always been my angel, cared for my dog and made sure my bills were paid. She often stayed with my brother and sister-in-law, whose transatlantic prayers over the phone each night when I relayed Kim's daily progress gave me comfort and hope to face yet another day of challenges.

When Kim was finally able to leave the ICU in January and begin physical rehabilitation at the hospital, she suffered a major pulmonary embolism caused by an undetected blood clot. Again, she nearly died and spent another two weeks in the ICU in critical condition, while on powerful anticoagulants. I'll never forget the image of four doctors and nurses on the day of her release from the ICU this second time, pushing her hospital bed out into the general hospitalization wing, smiling and wishing her well as she waved and said her goodbyes. They called her "La Reina (The Queen) of Intensive Care."

Today Kim is in good health, and works as an administrative assistant at a metabolic disease research center in Barcelona. She married the love of her life, Manuel ("Manu"), who was her next-door neighbor when they first met. Manu also had to rebuild his life, following a disastrous motorcycle accident several years earlier. They both feel that God has given them a second chance to live and they never take a single new day for granted. Kim and her husband now have a beautiful two-year-old son, Nicholas ("Nico"), who is the light of their lives.

The entire experience has strengthened our faith and forever changed our lives. So many miracles . . .so many angels sent in the form of family members, friends, neighbors and even random strangers . . .and so many prayers answered! God is so good!

— *Sue Katte*

thirty-eight

The Mysterious Stranger

Help me O Lord my God; save me according to
Your loving kindness, and let them know that this
is Your hand; You, Lord, have done it.
— Psalms 109:26-27

MY STORY BEGAN TWENTY-FIVE years ago when I was a young man. I lived at home with my mother. My father died earlier that year.

I worked in a factory, and it was time for our annual Christmas party. I really didn't want to go to the Christmas party that evening, but my friends were there, so I decided to go. Some of the finest food you have ever tasted was served at the party. The drinks were free of charge.

I thought I was invincible. I drank quite heavily that night and eventually became intoxicated. When the party broke up, we all went home.

When I saw my church on the ride home, I decided to get off the bus. I thought I would stop, say a prayer, and wish my dad a Merry Christmas. I was so intoxicated that I left my coat on the bus. The church was locked. I started to leave until I noticed a shrine of our Blessed Mother Mary outside the church. I knelt down to pray and, during my prayer, I passed out. It was quite cold. I fell asleep for what I would estimate was about one hour.

A man woke me up, telling me I would freeze to death if I did not get up. I did as he suggested, and I began to wake up. I was quite frozen. The man asked me where I lived, so I told him. I also told him that I did not want to go home looking like I did. I admitted that I was embarrassed to have my mother see me this way. So he suggested we both go to a restaurant, get something to eat, and then I clean up in the restroom. I agreed.

We began talking as we walked to the restaurant. He let me use his coat to warm up. When we got to the restaurant, I said, "Come in, so I can buy you some coffee. I do owe you at least that." The man refused, saying that he had other things to do that night. I said, "Okay." I thanked him for saving me from the cold and from myself. We said goodbye to each other. When I stepped into the restaurant, I realized that I was still wearing his coat. I turned around to give it back to him, but he was gone.

There was nowhere for him to go! The stores were all closed. I looked around ... **He was gone!**

So I went in, ate, cleaned up, and went home. When I woke up the next day, I still had the coat, so I knew it was not a dream. I remember it as if it were yesterday.

Now, twenty-five years later, I still can not explain it. Was that man my father watching over me? Was this person my guardian angel? Could this have been Jesus Himself? I don't know who that person was, but I thank whoever it was for watching over me that evening.

During my youth, whenever I would start to doubt my faith just a little, I would remember what happened that night. It always straightened me out. I never forgot and never will! Someone was watching out for me that night. **I still thank you, whoever you were!**

— *Ron Madl*

thirty-nine

The 14ᵗʰ Hole

And He will send forth His angels with a
great trumpet and they will gather together
His elect from the four winds, from one end
of the sky to the other.

— Matthew 24:31

I N THE WINTER OF 2004, Fr. Bob McLaughlin, a Chicago priest, was enjoying a winter vacation in Florida. He was playing golf with a married couple. At the 12th hole he experienced a pain in his chest, but he dismissed it as indigestion. At the 14th hole he slumped from the golf cart and lay unconscious on the ground. CPR was administered to him at once and he revived. He looked up at the sky and asked, "What's an angel doing on a golf course?" He then died at the age of sixty-two.

It's a traditional belief that, at the end of life, an angel is sent to God's elect to escort them to God. Fr. McLaughlin truly was blessed at the moment of his death.

SECTION SIX

Signs from the Deceased

・ forty ・

Feathers from an Angel

Blessed are those who mourn,
for they shall be comforted.
— Matthew 5:4

THERE ARE TINY DROPLETS of tears nestled behind my eyes that I know will never dry. On April 22, 2004, our daughter Linda, who was still in a coma after nine days, lay dying as our Lord called her home. As I held her in my arms during those final hours, an exceptional thought occurred to me. Consumed by feelings of anguish and desperation, I heard a voice speak. It was my voice. "Please, please Lindi, if possible, somehow let us know you are safe and not afraid . . . that you are okay and in the Lord's care." I wasn't cognizant enough to realize that my faith should be reassurance enough that she was soon to be in God's care and was in truth about to begin her journey home. As I watched her slip away, my grief was so overwhelming that I blurted out, "If you could but send me a feather, then I'd know you aren't frightened and that you're safe."

The following November my husband, Hermann, and I were boarding a bus bound for O'Hare Airport. As my husband dealt with the loading of our baggage outside, I went on a totally empty bus to settle in with a few of our "carry alongs." For some unexplained reason, I hesitated by two different sets of empty seats and chose not to sit down. As I approached another pair of empty seats, I stopped in my tracks. Lying there were two beautiful, perfectly shaped pheasant feathers. I could hardly breathe and stood there in total amazement. My husband and I had raised our daughters in an extended family. Their maternal grandmother had lived with us for forty-one years, was very close to my husband and me, as well as her three granddaughters, and had passed away six months prior to our daughter's death. As soon as my husband boarded the bus and saw the feathers he said, "Perhaps two feathers mean that both our daughter and her grandmother are safe and with our Lord."

We have come to realize that, with or without feathers, it is our faith in God the Father, Jesus His Son, and the Holy Spirit that will sustain us. Through His love we will someday be called home and shall see our loved ones. Then, and only then, will our arms stop aching to hold them and our hearts stop hurting. Until then, we have loved ones here on earth to whom we shall channel our energy and continue to give our unconditional love. As for us, the rest of our life here on earth, my husband and I need to prepare for our own journey home.

Unpublished Copyright © 2009—Barbara Opels-Mueller

forty-one

Frank

*"If therefore your whole body is full of
light, with no dark part in it, it will be
wholly illuminated, as when the lamp
illumines you with its rays."*

— Luke 11:36

MY LOVING HUSBAND, FRANK, was always a faith-filled person. As a child he loved going to church. Later in life Frank became a Eucharistic minister, liturgy team member, head sacristan, an usher, and a business manager at Transfiguration Parish in Wauconda, Illinois. He volunteered many times to serve food on Holy Thursday potluck dinner at St. Edna Parish in Arlington Heights, Illinois. Frank also had a desire to become a deacon, but this did not happen.

In 1992 Frank was preparing the bathroom for wallpaper. He fell off the ladder and broke his arm. Paramedics took him to the hospital. They set his arm and sent him home.

A day or two later, the hospital called and said they found a spot on Frank's lung. As advised, he went for tests. The results revealed a cancerous spot, which the doctor believed was curable and operable. Surgery was performed, and the lower lobe of the lung was removed. The doctor said that if the cancer returned, it would probably be located in the brain.

Frank was checked monthly for a year and was cancer free. Therefore, the doctor said monthly checkups were no longer necessary. Instead, they now are every six months.

One night in 1994, we were out for the evening. Frank was not himself, so he went to the doctor and told him what was happening. The doctor sent him for a brain scan. That is when we got the horrible news. He had brain cancer.

For the next year, I took care of Frank at home, except for his last two weeks of life. With the help of hospice, I did my best to make him comfortable that year. Hospice said I had to make other arrangements for his care, because I was close to having a breakdown. I gave in and sent Frank to a nursing home. In two weeks, he was gone.

Frank passed away March 14, 1995, at 2 a.m. My son and I went to the nursing home after we received the news. When we arrived we went directly to his room. He looked so peaceful. I saw a halo circling his whole being. I knew he was with God.

On our way out, the nurse on duty called us over and told us about the woman in the room next to him. The nurse said that the woman brought her doll collection with her to the nursing home. In this collection she had an angel doll that could light up and flap its wings if turned on. From time to time, the woman would call the nurse to her room and ask her to turn on the angel doll. The nurse said, "It was not easy to turn on." The patient told the nurse that at the exact moment Frank passed away, the doll lit up and flapped its wings. My son and I looked at each other with amazement before we left. I do believe the good Lord works in strange ways.

forty-two

The Class Ring

"Ask, and it will be given to you; seek and you will find; knock, and it will be opened to you. For everyone who asks receives, and he who seeks finds, and to him who knocks it will be opened.

— Matthew 7:7-8

SOMETIME IN EARLY SUMMER of 2002, my daughter Sarah lost her class ring while she was volunteering at the Veterans of Foreign Wars Friday evening fish fry. She thought it was in the pocket of the apron she was wearing.

The woman who washed the aprons went through all the clothes she washed in that load, and looked in the washer and dryer, but couldn't find the ring. My husband looked all over the VFW kitchen and couldn't find it either.

Then a co-worker of mine told me she had once lost an expensive earring, and had searched the entire house for it, but couldn't find it. So, she jokingly asked her deceased mother to find it and did not expect it would happen. The next day she saw something shiny in the carpet, and there was the earring.

She asked me if I had anyone recently die in my family. I said, "Yes, my mother died last August."

She asked, "Why don't you ask your dead mother to help you find the ring?"

That night on my way home, I asked Mom to look for Sarah's ring.

Early the next morning, the lady who washed the aprons called. She said that she found the ring in the lint screen, though it wasn't there when she had checked before. I could hardly believe my ears. I know that Mom found that ring!

— Holly Restemayer

forty-three

A Gift from Kouros

He who did not spare His own Son, but
delivered Him over for us all, how will He
not also with Him freely give us all things?
— Romans 8:32

I LOST MY SEVENTEEN-YEAR-OLD son in October of 2002. The void and sadness are unimaginable. I was in complete shock for awhile. All I wanted to do was die, so I would not have to endure the suffering. No parent should experience the loss of a child, but every day parents around the world are losing their children for different reasons.

I was on leave of absence for three and a half months. I returned to work late in January of 2003. I worked every day. I was consumed by so much grief that I tried to keep busy at work so I wouldn't spend so much time thinking about the tragedy.

One day when I was at work, I came back to my desk after taking a short break and saw a pin on my desk. It had an angel on the top and a blue oval shape on the bottom. The warmth of your fingers would cause an angel to appear on the stone when you held it.

I asked my co-workers if they knew who had put this pin on my desk. No one had seen anyone near my desk. I asked a few close friends at work to find out if any of them had given me the pin. They all said, "No."

I wear the pin most of the time. When I am driving and it is a sunny day, the angel glows when the sun comes through the windshield.

I never found out who gave me the pin. It is beautiful! I feel it is from my son Kouros.

—*Alieh Sadati*

• forty-four •

Dad's Plant

A time to give birth and a time to die; a time to plant and a time to uproot what is planted.

— Ecclesiastes 3:2

DAD NEVER WAS MUCH for working in the yard, landscaping, or growing things. I never even heard him mention a flower or plant that he found particularly interesting or attractive. Growing flowers was something other people did, not my dad. That was okay with him. He had other things to do. He was a master at fixing just about anything that broke. That must have been why when he decided to plant the clematis our whole family was surprised. For whatever reason, on that particular day, with a small clematis vine in hand, dad picked up a shovel, walked over to a formerly unproductive plot of land by the house, dug around in the dirt, and stuck the plant squarely in the center of the hole. To make the whole process even more amazing to us, he secured a trellis right next to the plant with absolute confidence that eventually that little plant would need help to keep it upright and strong. And sure enough, in just a short time, the clematis just took off. It grew, it blossomed, and it took on a life of its own year after year. It was magnificent! Dad loved that plant that had now become a vine, abundant with giant purple blossoms. It was "Dad's plant" and he was very proud of it.

I grew up and eventually moved to another town hundreds of miles away from home. Whenever I saw a clematis growing in a yard near mine, I would smile and think of Dad and replay the day he just put that little plant in the ground. Visiting home each year, I marveled at the tenacity of that plant and the special attention Dad had given it.

One year, I was summoned home. It was apparent that Dad was gravely ill. After a long, difficult illness, Dad left us. Several days after his funeral, it was time to leave the home I grew up in to return to my own home. It was the hardest thing I'd ever done. How was I going to leave my memories of Dad? How was I going to leave him buried here and still keep him with me in my heart and in my own home?

Weeks after the funeral, I was still grieving for my father. One spring morning, I sat on the porch of my home, missing Dad. My heart was heavy. I needed to feel him there with me. I needed more than just my heartaches and memories. It was then I remembered the plant he loved. I thought about how he just decided one day that he needed to have it and how important it was to him. I decided I'd do exactly what he did. That very afternoon, I bought a clematis plant. Now, a green thumb I'm not. Like Dad, the art of gardening eluded me. Undeterred, I simply did what he did. I dug around in the dirt, placed the plant in the hole, and secured a trellis next to it. I watered the puny little thing and silently prayed that Dad would take good care of it. I left my hope in God's hands.

Time passed. All the other gardens in the neighborhood became flooded with color. Gardens bloomed. My plant, though tall and green, wasn't looking like Dad's. In fact, there wasn't one purple blossom to be seen. All summer I waited and longed for his plant to bloom, but it never did. The same was true the following spring. When all the other gardens danced with color, the vine looked healthy and strong, but not one blossom appeared.

Dad's birthday was nearing. I was feeling particularly lonely for him. I really hadn't paid much attention to my "Dad's plant" because it just wasn't doing what I'd hoped. It didn't look at all like the one Dad had planted. I had spent some time in prayer thinking of Dad when I happened to look at his plant early one morning—only to notice a bud burgeoning from the vine! I was ecstatic! Finally, my plant was going to look like his! Then, on his birthday, as his special gift to me, that plant produced the biggest, most beautiful purple blossom I could have hoped for. Looking at the flower, I could see my dad smiling and could feel him with me. I could hear his voice and the funny songs he used to sing. I could feel his pride and believed that it was his special way of letting me know he would always be with me, even when I couldn't see him, hold him, or tell him I loved him. His gift to me was wonderful—and I wanted more. I wanted mounds of beautiful flowers all the time. I wanted to tell everyone that Dad was in charge of this plant. I wanted everyone to see just how gorgeous he was making it for me. But, what I wanted just didn't happen.

Instead, my dad did something I needed even more. No, my plant didn't grow and become abundant when everyone else's plants did. Instead, Dad gave me a plant that produced magnificent blooms just twice a year—once on his birthday and once again on Father's Day.

It's been many years that "Dad's plant" has given me beauty, grace, and comfort. Twice a year, when I miss him most, I can find him in the beauty of his plant. Last year, a deep frost made it impossible for Dad's plant to grow. While I miss it, I have to wonder if Dad knew that I'd be okay and that I wouldn't need it the way I needed it years ago.

In any case, I am truly grateful to have known the goodness of my father. He loved me and knew I needed to know he would always be there for me. He kept showing me just how much he cared, even after he was gone, in that beautiful plant I always called "Dad's plant" . . . and isn't that just like the beauty, love, and care of our Heavenly Father's love?

— *Kathryn Marchioni Davy*

forty-five

Our Little E.L.F.

But Jesus said, "Let the children alone, and do not hinder them from coming to Me; for the kingdom of heaven belongs to such as these."

— Matthew 19:14

ERIN LOUISE FITZGERALD WAS born July 31, 1998. She was a gift from God to my sister, Michele, and my brother-in-law, Bruce. Erin soon came to be known as "Sunshine" to everyone that met her and knew her. She would walk into a room and just talk to anyone who would listen to her. A few people have commented that they were so excited to talk to her and so energized by her mood.

Erin had a normal first four years, until August 2002. At a family gathering, she began to drool from the side of her mouth, and she did not move her right arm very much. A few of us noticed this and asked my sister if she had been ill. My sister said, "No, she has been fine; maybe she is just tired."

For better or worse, I am a nurse, and I think like a nurse. I checked her out a bit and told my sister she needed to get her checked out soon; this is not normal. Erin also began to choke on her water. I knew there was something seriously wrong. She was behaving like a stroke victim.

My sister agreed to take her to the doctor in the morning if she wasn't any better. I left that night and told my husband on the way home that I thought she had a brain tumor.

My sister called the next day and told us she had taken Erin to the ER early in the morning. The doctors were not sure what was wrong, especially because Erin's symptoms had disappeared. She told me that they were doing a urine test because they thought it might be an infection.

I more or less yelled at my sister to stress that they **needed** to do a CT scan of her brain, and she said she would insist on it.

We received a call back a few hours later; they had found a relatively large tumor in Erin's brain, in an area that is called the pons. The name of the tumor is "pons glioma." The pons controls breathing and pretty much all bodily functions. It seemed the tumor was pushing on the left side of her brain; therefore, she had weakness on her right side.

Erin was transported via ambulance to Children's Memorial in Chicago, since this rural hospital could not help her. Unfortunately, surgeons were only able to tell us bad news. No one survived this type of brain tumor, and surgery was impossible due to its location. To say this was traumatic is putting it mildly. Words could not be found to describe the pain Erin's parents felt—we all were in pain.

Time passed, and Erin went home. She then went to radiation every day for six weeks and had chemotherapy. At one hospital visit, my aunt stayed with her overnight to give my sister and brother-in-law a break. Erin desperately wanted her play doh. My aunt looked, to no avail. It could not be found. Erin was so upset she pushed the call light for the nurse. The nurse came in, and when she asked her what she needed, Erin said: "I need my play doh!" Erin was so persistent that the nurse even helped look for it! She finally found it and all was well again.

Erin stayed with her mom at our brother's house during radiation since it was much closer. Erin was always the ray of sunshine, even when her hair fell out. She didn't care; she just wanted to play and eat her fishy crackers (Goldfish crackers). Erin said to my sister on more than one occasion, "Don't worry, Mom, I am not going to die."

Unfortunately, the story gets worse. My sister, Michele, and brother-in-law, Bruce, were visiting Erin at the hospital when my sister went to the restroom.

While she was in the restroom, she experienced the worst headache she had ever had. Then she went to the nurse's station and told them that she thought she had brain aneurysm.

Michele was taken to the ER at Children's. She promptly passed out and was transported, via ambulance, to nearby Northwestern University. She nearly died from an AVM (arteriovenous malformation) in her brain. This is similar to an aneurysm, but it is something one is born with and consists of a large cluster of tangled arteries and veins in the brain. My sister was trapped at Northwestern, and her baby was at Children's.

It appears that if Erin had not been at Children's on that day, my sister very well may have died. Michele lives far from these wonderful hospitals, and the rural hospital may not have had the tools to help her fast enough.

Erin became sicker and sicker. We had hospice called in at her home, since Erin hated going to the hospital, and the doctors felt it really wasn't going to help her anymore. We had many nights of prayer; we would all stand over her and pray out loud. Erin was nearly comatose at that time; she was unresponsive to all of us. But when we prayed, Erin would open her eyes, hold her arms up, and "talk" to someone; she often would say, "Yes, I see you." Once we stopped praying, she would return to her previous unresponsive state.

Erin had her last Christmas in 2002. Her mom was in the hospital, and Erin was with the rest of us. We all opened presents with my sister on the phone, listening to all that was going on. The videotape we made of this Christmas is irreplaceable! It was the best Christmas ever—it taught us the two most important things in life are family and loving each other.

My sister came home from the hospital, with just enough time to be with Erin before she died. We all felt the power of God there with us. It was very intense, but peaceful.

Erin was only here a few short years, but I can tell you she touched all of our lives in so many ways. There are some people who are alive for many, many years, and they do not burn a memory in our hearts and minds the way that Erin did.

About one year later, Erin's cousin was at home playing. He was very close to Erin since they were only a few months apart in age.

He had come in the room and said to his mom, "Erin was here, we were playing for a while, and then she said she had to go."

His mom was baffled and said, "How is she?"

He said, "She was fine. She has come to visit before." He then went off to play.

Perhaps the most amazing thing about all of this is that Erin was adopted. My sister and brother-in-law had tried for many years to get pregnant with fertility medications and in vitro fertilization. She became pregnant twice and lost both babies within a few weeks. The neurosurgeon had told my sister that, had she ever given birth, she would have died at childbirth due to the pressure buildup in her brain from the AVM. Erin had once again been her mom's savior. We felt that she was an angel sent here to save her mother's life.

Ironically, Erin's favorite song was "Soak up the Sun" by Sheryl Crow. We played it at her funeral. We also played a bunch of videotapes that our families had compiled. The videotapes remind us how truly special Erin was; these too are irreplaceable.

I am sharing this story about my special niece Erin to honor her memory. I have also begun a foundation for pediatric brain tumor research. Donations may be sent to:

> *Erin Louise Fitzgerald Foundation*
> *(ELF Foundation)*
> *C/O Diane Ayers*
> *261 North Fremont Street*
> *Palatine, Illinois 60067*

Now that my sister, Michele, has recovered from her brain injury, she has taken the reins and will continue to pursue finding a cure for this devastating pediatric cancer.

— *Diane Ayers*

forty-six

Heavenly Hospital Visitors

For the wage of sin is death, but the free gift of
God is eternal life in Christ Jesus our Lord.

— Romans 6:23

WHEN JULIA WAS DIAGNOSED with colon cancer at age eighty-one, there was some evidence that metastasis had already occurred. Still, the doctor felt there was hope that the colostomy she underwent could be reversed if chemotherapy and radiation treatments were effective.

Julia went through all therapies courageously, suffering side effects with hope and even humor—one of her best qualities. She was a woman of great faith who with her husband had reared eight children and was grandmother to many more. She never lost hope for a cure.

A year later she even elected to risk her immediate death by deciding to go ahead with one more procedure. But then the doctor declined, citing professional ethics. She was sent home to the care of her family along with hospice support.

Julia felt her faith flag because she had done everything she could in life to serve God, and now God was letting her and her husband down. Why weren't her prayers answered in the way she wanted? Why couldn't she live longer?

With medication she was without pain during her last week on earth, and she still asked why God would not help her overcome this disease. Then one day, with her daughter and son-in-law present on either side of her bed, she opened her eyes and said, "I see Jesus."

Her husband, George, who was at the foot of the bed and hard of hearing, did not hear this. Her son-in-law asked quickly, "What did you say?"

"I see Jesus Christ," she whispered. Opening her eyes once more, she then drifted off to sleep and died peacefully the next day.

The devoted family felt this was a great grace for them. Mom had lived her religion, but with so much suffering it was hard to see her faith tested so long. Their faith was tested as well because it was so difficult to see her suffer. The gift of peace came to all of them through her vision.

I was dozing in a chair while visiting my dying mother, Dorothy, near her hospital bedside. I don't know if you can call my experience a vision or a dream. It was only a split second or two. This could even be more of my imagination than anything else. I never got a good look at any faces. But for just a second, I could see a row of people all in white sitting as if this were a movie. The only person I recognized in the group was my mother's deceased cousin Regina. (Regina would frequently bike ride to Dorothy's home. Over the years Dorothy was a sympathetic friend when Regina needed support, and now Regina was comforting Dorothy in her transition to death.) That is when I said, "Mom, they are all waiting for you." It was a peaceful feeling even if it was in my mind. I do believe it did help me to get through the passing.

The next day my cousin, Sarah, called to tell me her dream about Dorothy with hope that it would comfort me. Sarah also mentioned that she had never dreamt of Dorothy before. She saw my mother with a look of incredible happiness on her face. I was overwhelmed with joy.

A seventy-five-year-old woman had been struggling for years with chronic heart failure. On her last trip to the hospital the staff had a lot of trouble getting her off the respirator because she was terrified of dying. Finally, she was successfully weaned from the respirator and was sent home in the care of her daughters. She would barely let her daughters out of her sight.

That evening she told the daughter present that her deceased son was there. She became absolutely calm. Her daughter asked her where he was, and she replied that he was standing at the foot of the bed. Then she fell asleep quietly.

When the other daughter came in to take over, the mother awoke again and told her daughters that their father was also present and that they should pray for her because she wanted to go with them. Within the hour she died peacefully.

When my grandfather was seventy-four years old he became very ill. Ten years earlier he had one kidney removed. He was on dialysis and near death.

Our immediate family was called to his hospital bedside. We gathered around him and sometimes sat on his bed. Grandpa was in a coma.

Suddenly Grandpa opened his eyes, smiled, and began to speak in Italian. I asked my father what he was saying. He said, "Grandpa is speaking to his mother!"

Grandpa lapsed back into a coma. The next day he died while I was at work. Some family members were present. We all knew that Grandpa had a heavenly visitor.

forty-seven

Amazing Happenings

Thus do I pour out instructions like prophecy and
bestow it on generations to come.

— Sirach 24:31 NAB

ALL OF THESE HAPPENINGS occurred following my husband's death. My husband Dave died on May 13, 2003.

The first of these unusual experiences happened while I was sitting in a small room, in a hospital in Kansas City, waiting for the birth of my son's second son. I was all alone. The day this happened was July 11, 2003, just a few months after the death of my dear husband. All of a sudden, I heard a voice say, "He is here and he is fine." I looked at the clock and noted that it was 8:17 a.m. Little David James Cunningham was born at exactly 8:17 a.m. I thanked Dave.

My second happening occurred on the last Christmas we celebrated together. My husband gave me a pair of pearl earrings. One day I wore the earrings to work. During the course of the day, I noticed one was missing. I was really upset and looked all over the office, the car, and my bedroom. I could not find it. I was very disappointed that I could not find the earring, and I gave up the cause.

The next day I walked to work. When I came to the corner to push the walk light, I decided to move two feet to the slope in the curb and wait there. I guess I did this just for something to do because it is a very long light. I looked down at the gutter and there, surrounded by tiny pebbles and dirt, was my earring. I thanked Dave.

My third story took place in northern Wisconsin at a hunting and fishing preserve called Smokey Game Preserve. Our entire family went to the preserve, but mostly my late husband Dave went there with a group of men. They call themselves the "Boys of October."

Last October, the "Boys of October" met for their usual day of shooting birds. When they were finished they all went their separate ways. Some went to town, one went fishing, and one took a nap. They agreed to meet later for dinner.

The man who was sleeping, Mike, was trying to rest when a very bright light disturbed him. He rolled over and tried to fall asleep again, but the light reappeared. He got up angrily, walked into the living room, and looked out the window. That is when he suddenly noticed that his friend who had gone fishing had fallen out of the boat and was struggling in the water.

Mike ran to the end of the long pier and told his friend to stay at the boat. That boat was the only one on the lake. He told him he would run to get help. Mike ran back to the cabin and called the main gate. For some unknown reason, all of the staff was present in the office and they all raced to help. The man was rescued.

The next day the entire group went to church. They all thanked Dave.

— *Cecile Cunningham*

forty-eight

Heaven's Fairway

*So also is the resurrection of the dead. It is sown a perishable
body, it is raised an imperishable body; it is sown in dishonor, it is
raised in glory; it is sown in weakness, it is raised in power; it is
sown a natural body, it is raised a spiritual body.*

— 1 Corinthians 15:42

MY DAD, WILL, WAS passionate about golf and regarded his hole-in-one trophy ball as one of his most prized possessions. Who would ever imagine that one day he would use this recognizable symbol to communicate with us from the other side?

The last several months of their more than fifty-six years of marriage were trying times for my parents, who were faced with my dad's sudden illness, a rare form of cancer, and his imminent death. The illness robbed him of his favorite pursuits, one by one, including his beloved golf game. Though he could no longer join his buddies in their customary round of eighteen holes, he would occasionally ride part of the way with them in the golf cart, basking in the uplifting camaraderie the outing provided.

Much of his time was now spent in doctors' offices and dealing with his digestive problems in the bathroom. To make his time in the lavatory less unpleasant, I decorated the room in a golfing motif, with photos of lush greens and golfers teeing off and putting, and I hung a wall clock that featured a golf ball pendulum.

Dad knew he didn't have much time left, and this strong hero of a man told me, with tears in his eyes, "I'm not afraid of dying; I just don't want to leave my family."

I reassured him he would be with us a long time, but I didn't believe my own words. I told him he had to promise me that, if he did leave us at some point, he would try to send us a sign from heaven that he was all right and still with us in spirit. He promised he would try his hardest.

During that holiday season in 2001, Dad's condition rapidly deteriorated. Hospice workers, who assisted my mom in her round-the-clock care of my dad, were loving and patient people. Mom certainly lived out her "in sickness and in health" vow during those difficult times. On Christmas Day, I lifted my formerly muscular, tall father into a chair and wheeled him into the living room. For two or three hours, he was lucid, witty, and wise. We had a wonderful chat about nearly everything under the sun! What a blessing that conversation with him was, as that was our last talk before he slipped into a coma-like sleep. His goal was to make it through Christmas, and he did just that. He passed into eternal life on Dec. 27, with my mother Betty, my brother Bill, and me at his bedside.

Mom managed her grief through purposeful activity and began to get her house in Wheaton, Illinois, ready to sell just a few months later. Dad would have loved the beautiful townhouse she bought in Buffalo Grove, near my Palatine home in the northwest suburbs of Chicago. Mementos of his wonderful life were given a special place of honor on top of the entertainment center—his military medals from the Marines; the veteran's triangular-folded flag, presented to my mom at his funeral; family photos; and, of course, his hole-in-one trophy, next to his ever- smiling portrait. Mom often claimed she could see Dad's lips moving in the picture, as though he were talking to her.

Dad's prize golf ball had sat proudly for years in a stand, anchored firmly in place. Now it rested, just as securely, in Mom's new home. One night, Mom was alone, reading in the living room. Her neighborhood was quiet—the only sound was the reassuring tick of the mantle clock. Suddenly, the golf ball fell out of its cradle, bounced off the top of the cabinet, and rolled on the carpet toward my mother. No airplane had passed overhead, the street was dark, and there were no vibrations from outside or next door. She picked up the ball and replaced it in its stand. Within a few minutes, the ball again bounced down and rolled toward her on the sofa. Terrified, Mom left the golf ball on the carpet, hurried into her bedroom, and closed the door to spend a nearly sleepless night.

The next day she told me what had happened and asked me to come over and put the ball back, this time taped in place. As I followed her request, I remembered Dad's promise to contact us from heaven and was excited to think that he had chosen this novel way to communicate with us! Looking at Dad's smiling portrait, I told him he had frightened Mom with his little friendly gesture, but I wanted him to know that I would love for him to come to me in any way he'd like. To this day he hasn't, except in dreams, but my eyes, ears, mind, and heart are open to the experience. Dad always kept his promises, even from heaven!

— *Susan Katte*

forty-nine

Our Angel Teresa

Love is patient, love is kind and is not jealous; love does not brag
and is not arrogant, does not act unbecomingly; it does not seek its
own, is not provoked, does not take into account a wrong suffered,
does not rejoice in unrighteousness, but rejoices with the truth; bears
all things, believes all things, hopes all things, endures all things.

— 1 Corinthians 13:4-7

NINETEEN YEARS AGO, ON January 17, 1993, my granddaughter, Teresa, dramatically came into this world. She was rushed out of the delivery room, put into an ambulance, and sent to Loyola Medical Center. Her mother went home to her two children, and her father followed the ambulance.

For the next year no one knew if Teresa would make it because of problems relating to her brain. The picture was grim, but Teresa made it through. She truly blessed our lives by living nine years and four days and was a wonderful gift from God.

Teresa suffered seizures until she was two years old. Only minor and periodic seizures occurred after that. A shunt was inserted shortly after birth because of water on her brain: a condition known as hydrocephalus.

She would never sit alone, stand, walk, or learn to talk. The only word she said was, "Da." She'd make sounds, especially when music was on. She loved music, and the family played special tapes for her over and over.

Michael was Teresa's closest cousin and was younger than Teresa. He was four years old when Teresa died. When the family would get together at Grandpa's house, Teresa would sit on the rug surrounded by her musical toys. She had a favorite musical toy, which required her to press the *On* button to start different songs. Michael would lie down on the rug and press the *Off* button just to see what Teresa would do. As soon as the music stopped, Teresa would run her hand over the *On* button and get it started again. Michael got a big kick out of it and started laughing. He could approach her and enjoy her comfortably.

After the funeral, which Michael did not attend, Michael was told that Teresa died. From then on, he would always ask where she was. His mother would reply, "She is in heaven with God." Michael wasn't happy with that answer and asked why God didn't send her back. He was told that God couldn't do that. After thinking for a while, Michael announced that he didn't like God.

After some time passed, Michael and his mother were riding in their car when he began talking about Teresa. Michael told his mother, "Teresa is happy."

His mother said, "How do you know?"

Michael said, "She told me when I talked to her."

Two months after Teresa died, Teresa's mom, Kathy, awoke from her sleep one night. Although her eyes were closed, she felt that someone was there. She put her left hand up and felt a warm breath and clay-like head. Thinking it was a male, she was afraid to open her eyes, but she had to open her eyes in case it was Teresa. No one was there, or was she?

Teresa's mom was in the family room with her son Steven. The two remote controls were on the couch in front of Kathy. The sound remote, which controls the tape, was off, but somehow the tape started playing.

To get the tape to play you have to press three different buttons. No one was near the remote. It had to be Teresa.

Another time Kathy was sleeping. She woke up suddenly to see Teresa's toy piano glowing different colors: purple, red, and orange. It kept changing colors, which were very bright. Teresa loved banging on this piano. Kathy guessed this was caused by the moonlight coming through the window. Later, however, she realized that this wouldn't have accounted for the different colors. Teresa was giving her a sign.

Every second weekend of the month, Teresa would stay at our home and would sleep with us. After she died, I often felt someone moving on the bed. I would jump up and check to see if there was anyone there, and I could feel that Teresa was there visiting us.

Every once in a while one of the paintings I've made of Teresa falls off the wall. I know she is letting me know she will always be with us. She is!

On January 7, 2005, I had an appointment to have my teeth cleaned. When I arrived I told my hygienist, Heidi, that Teresa's birthday was coming up. She asked me if we were going to celebrate her birthday. I said that we were. I told Heidi that I was going to make a cake and take it to the gravesite. Then I told Heidi the story about Michael playing with Teresa after she had died. I mentioned to Heidi that Michael told his parents that Teresa said she is happy.

As Heidi cleaned my teeth, she told me some of the stories that were already in the book. Then she stood up to get some floss. When she turned around to face me, she could see large tears rolling down my cheeks. She said, "I am sorry to have stirred up sad memories for you."

I said, "No, that is not it, that is not it at all . . . I just saw her. I just saw Teresa. Her face was right in front of me. Her face was glowing; it was radiant. I saw every detail of her face. I haven't been able to picture those details for over three years." I couldn't wait to leave the dental office to tell my daughter about the vision of Teresa.

❀

Teresa died unexpectedly. We thought she would be with us for thirty years. She was such a happy, loving child. While she was with us, we felt that we were living with an angel.

— *Kathy Hoover*
and
Grandma Pat Kantecki

fifty

The Butterfly and the Doves

John testified saying, "I have seen the Spirit
descending as a dove out of heaven, and He
remained on him.

— John 1:32

ABOUT NINE YEARS AGO, my good friend, who had been sick with cancer for a long time, lost his battle. After his wife and son had made all the funeral arrangements, they were walking into their backyard when the wife expressed the wish: if only she had a sign her husband was all right. Just then a butterfly landed right on her heart. The butterfly did not move away even as she moved to wipe her tears.

In time, the wife also died. One day, I felt especially sad that they were gone. I looked out my window and saw two doves sitting on my flower box. We have never seen doves on our windowsill before or since. I said a few prayers for them and told the doves it was okay. I know they are together and are safe.

fifty-one

L-U-C-I-L-L-E

Jesus said to her, "I am the resurrection and the life; he who believes in Me will live even if he dies, and everyone who lives and believes in Me will never die. Do you believe this?"

— John 11: 25-26

SOMETIME IN THE YEAR 2000, a mother and daughter went to the Queen of Heaven Cemetery in Chicago to visit her grandmother's grave. She was very close to her departed grandmother Lucille. She quite often would go to the mausoleum to say a few prayers for both of her grandparents.

This time, she brought along a picture of her twin daughters and taped it to the front of their crypt. Just as she did this three letters from Lucille's name fell to the floor. When she picked them up, she was shocked to see they were the letters I-C-U.

In a much shaken state, she brought the letters to the main office so they could be replaced. When the secretary heard the story, she too was taken aback.

Healing

fifty-two

Healing Experience

For from Him and through Him and to Him are
all things. To Him be the glory forever. Amen.

— Romans 11:36

IN 1984, I WAS a twenty-year-old man in my junior year, studying health care administration at the University of Illinois, when I developed unusual health problems. I came down with numerous symptoms: constant fatigue, tremors, and enlarged lymph nodes and spleen. Over the next year, I visited numerous physicians (about ten specialists, including specialists at the University of Chicago). I experienced a variety of diagnostic tests, which included CT scans, biopsies, bone marrow, and a splenectomy. Thousands of dollars of expense were incurred for all of these medical tests, all in an effort to find some answers for my collection of symptoms. Yet, no answers were ever found.

During this time I began to wonder seriously about my eternal destiny. After a clear presentation of the Gospel, I trusted Jesus Christ as my Savior. This removed fears about my eternal destiny, but my medical symptoms remained unabated.

Over the next few months I prayed more often. The Lord began to convict me about my need to grow in Him. During this time, I did grow spiritually, and at the end of some intensive Bible study the Lord made it very clear to me that He wanted me to go on a short-term missions trip. This direction seemed impossible since I was still sleeping about twelve hours per day and feeling awful during my waking hours. Nevertheless, the Spirit of God was compelling me to go, so I made plans to do so.

I remember having a repentant heart and **committing myself to serve God wherever He would lead**. This is something I expressed before I was healed. God had given me the confidence that I would be healed. I should add that I have not experienced that kind of confidence since. It is as though He was giving me the ability to thank Him because He had already given me the assurance that He was going to heal me.

The next week, after I made plans to attend the missions trip, and the weeks to follow, my condition greatly improved. My need for sleep decreased, as did the constant tremors that I was having in my hands and legs. Two months later, during the missions trip, my symptoms were **gone** completely, never to return!

Upon my recovery, it was evident that what was necessary for healing was my submission to God in my life. Also, I was convinced that the world didn't need another health care administrator offering man-centered solutions but rather more people presenting the truth of God. For me, this meant entering seminary and then pastoral ministry.

— A Pastor from Florida

fifty-three

To Honor Padre Pio

Is anyone among you sick? Then he must call for the elders of the church and they are to pray over him, anointing him with oil in the name of the Lord; and the prayer offered in faith will restore the one who is sick, and the Lord will raise him up, and if he has committed sins, they will be forgiven.

— James 5:14-15

I WANT TO HONOR THE great Capuchin friar, St. Padre Pio of Foggia, Italy, with this amazing story. He performed a wonderful miracle for my family on July 18, 1976. I remember the date very well because we moved on Friday afternoon, which was the Holy day of our Lady of Mt. Carmel.

That Sunday, a friend of my oldest son came over and told us that my son, Steve, was in a car accident in Wisconsin. The accident wasn't too bad, but Steve's neck was injured. He said that Steve was holding his neck until the paramedics got there and that his ear was severely severed. Then the paramedics took him away. Wouldn't you know that our phone wasn't installed yet! That is why Steve's friend had to come to our new home to tell us about Steve's accident.

My other son, Tom, knew that I was very upset. He said, "Ma, I'll drive you because you are too upset." We were told Steve wasn't hurt that bad.

We decided to go to the car pound and take the stereo out of his car because it was very expensive. That was a big mistake. When we got to the place where they towed his car, we saw that every window in the car was out. The car was dented so badly that I almost passed out. I told Tom, "We have to go to Mc Henry Hospital in Richmond, Wisconsin."

We had driven about fifty-five miles by the time we reached the hospital in Wisconsin. It must have been about two hours when we finally arrived there. They moved my unconscious son from the Mc Henry Hospital to Northwestern Memorial Hospital in Chicago because his injuries were so severe. Steve's ear was almost completely severed. They couldn't take care of his neck because they weren't into handling that type of traumatic injury. That is when I realized how serious Steve's injuries really were!

It was one or two in the morning when we got to Northwestern Memorial Hospital. Tom was driving downtown about eighty miles an hour.

My husband was a fireman in River Forest and was on duty when he received the news about the accident. He was told to meet us at Northwestern Memorial Hospital.

Steve was moaning when I went into the room to see him. He said, "Tell them to give me something; I can't stand the pain." They had already fixed his ear and placed a bandage over it.

I thought that since Steve had been away from the church God would **not** help him! Then I started praying for a priest. It was one in the morning. I needed to get a priest to anoint my son in case he passed on.

Then a nurse came in and said, "You will have to leave because we are going to prep your son."

I said, "He is hurting so bad. Did you hear him?"

The nurse said, "We are going to have to drill into his skull without anesthesia; he will probably be hollering and screaming. So, you had better go wait in the lobby."

Before we went into the waiting room, I said, "Before you do anything, I want to see him." I told Steve, "I am going to touch you with Padre Pio's medal wherever you are hurting, and I am going to ask Jesus, Mary, and Padre Pio to heal you and help you." I used the Padre Pio medal I had on my rosary (I had received this medal directly from Padre Pio. I used to write him when he was alive.). I touched Steve's ear and legs. They couldn't give him anything because he was unconscious and they were afraid he would go into a coma. I found out his neck was broken. Two of Steve's vertebras were fractured. It was an injury similar to the injury Christopher Reeve suffered many years later.

I said to Stevie, "I will wait out in the hall with Tom. I will come back in when they take care of you." I went out into the vestibule. It was about two in the morning when I saw a priest in the corner. I went over to the priest and said, "Father, my son has been in a terrible accident. Would you anoint him? He has been away from the church."

He said, "No problem." The priest said he was called in to anoint the other boy who was in the room with my son. "I will anoint both of them."

I said, "Let me go in and tell Steve before you come in because he will think he is dying." I went into Steve's room and said, "Steve, there is a priest here. I asked him to anoint you. He will give you a blessing of the sick." I didn't tell him he would be given his last rites.

Then Steve said, "Okay, Mom whatever you say."

I left the room and the priest anointed Steve. The nurses said there was nothing more I could do. Meanwhile, my husband came to the hospital. We told Steve that we were going back to Schaumburg and would come back tomorrow.

The next day, I went to Mass at St. Marceline. At the petitions they asked if anyone wanted a petition for special prayers. Well, that is when I lost it and started sobbing. I kept saying, "Pray for my son, Steve, who was in a terrible accident. Could you pray for him?" After Mass many people came up to me and said that they would pray for Steve. They told me that they had a prayer group and that they would tell everyone to pray for Steve. Then I went to see him. In fact, we went every day for three weeks. He was in the intensive care ward for patients with neck injuries.

Steve was in a room with several other fellows. I asked one young man, "How did you get injured?" He told me that he jumped through an inner tube and hit the bottom of the pool. He couldn't move anything. He had a tray of food, so I asked him, "Do you want me to feed you?"

He said, "I would like my potatoes because they will get cold." So, I fed him his potatoes.

Then Steve mentioned later that all four patients in the room had neck injuries. Steve said, "I think God put me here so I could call the nurses because none of the other patients can move." About every hour, on the hour, they turned Steve so he wouldn't get blood clots. Steve learned how to eat upside down!

After the three weeks, they finally decided that they were going to fuse Steve's spine with bones from his hip. That meant, though, that he wouldn't be able to turn his head. He got so upset that he started to get ulcers from the worry.

I said, "I will pray for you all the time." I went to Mass every day.

He said, "Ma, I am going to have surgery on Monday."

I said, "I never got to see your doctor." He told me his doctor's name. When I went into the hall, I asked the nurse sitting there, "Do you know which doctor is going to operate on Steve?"

She said, "That is my husband, but he never comes here on a Thursday."

Steve was supposed to have surgery on the following Monday. When we came in on Monday, we found out that Steve did not have his surgery. I asked him, "Why didn't you have your surgery?"

He said, "They lost my X-rays."

I said, "They lost your X-rays in this big hospital?" I knew Padre Pio was already interceding.

We visited Steve every day. A new surgery date was scheduled for Friday. That Thursday I talked to the nurse again. She said her husband never comes because he is on call or at some kind of meeting. I said, "I just want to know what they are going to do to him tomorrow."

The nurse said, "No, I can't call him or anything. I can never disturb him because he is in a conference somewhere."

I said, "Okay."

Then I went back into the room with my husband. We were talking to Steve because he was getting very upset that he might not be able to move his neck. About one hour later, who comes in the room but Steve's doctor! He **never** comes in on Thursdays. He was smiling. I said, "Are you the doctor that is going to operate on my son?"

He said, "Yes. I have good news for you. We took new X-rays. He is healing so quickly that he does not need the surgery."

I said, "**Wow, that is great!**" I knew that Padre Pio was healing my son.

The doctor said, "He is doing so well that he can go home. We will put him in a neck brace. You can pick him up tomorrow. In three months, I want you to bring him back to see how everything is."

I said, "**Great!**" So, we took him home.

Three months later he went back. Meanwhile, his ear was almost healed. A German doctor checked him out. He asked, "Can you turn your head?" Steve turned it back and forth. Then the doctor asked, "Does that hurt?"

Steve said, "No."

The doctor said, "Man, are you lucky!"

Steve said, "I know it, and my mother will never let me forget it, either," and I won't.

One year later Steve got married. He and his wife now have three beautiful boys.

This is the wonderful story of the miracle that Padre Pio performed for my son Steve. Steve's ear healed so completely that they said it would feel as if nothing ever happened. He was completely healed: the neck, the ear, everything was healed. I am always so grateful to Padre Pio for what he did that I always try to spread devotion to him whenever I can. When beatification came I didn't get to go to that. I thought that maybe in a couple of years I would go to his canonization. So, that is when I prayed and thanked him at his tomb.

Here is another Padre Pio miracle story that I heard from a man at my church. He had prostate cancer and had been in the hospital prior to visiting Padre Pio's tomb in Italy. He was suffering so badly from cancer of the prostate that he said, "I don't think I can make the trip." He did, however, go to Italy with his wife.

He prayed for healing at Padre Pio's tomb. He said, "After I prayed at the tomb, I started feeling pretty good, and before that time I could hardly walk to the tomb."

Later that evening, when he and his wife went back to their room, his wife said, "You take the lower bunk."

He said, "No, I think I will take the top bunk." For three days, he never revealed that he was healed. Now he spreads devotion to Padre Pio.

— *Evelyn M. Daudelin*

For additional information on Padre Pio please contact:

The Capuchin Friars Minor
71013 San Giovanni Rotondo-Foggia (Italy)
Tel. 0039.0882.4171 Fax 0039.0882.417252

Web sites:
www.sanpiodapietrelcina.it
www.capuchinfriarypadrepio.com
www.conventopadrepio.it/com

E-mail:
cappuccini@conventopadrepio.com

Capuchin Franciscan Friars
P.O. Box 839
Union City, N. J. 07087-0839

fifty-four

A Mother's Faith

Now may the God of hope fill you with all joy and
peace in believing, so that you will abound in hope by
the power of the Holy Spirit.

— Romans 15:13

MY STORY BEGINS IN the fall of my son's eighth grade year in school. Tom was preparing to receive the Sacrament of Confirmation and graduate from elementary school.

All of a sudden, he developed a large growth on his forehead. The pediatrician, Dr. Perez, was not alarmed but advised having a plastic surgeon remove it. Tom went through outpatient surgery. We returned a week later to have the stitches removed. When we arrived, the doctor greeted us and then told us that the report showed that this was a cancerous tumor. I was shocked but did not want to overreact in front of Tom. The doctor said it was not skin cancer, but he could not adequately explain what this cancer involved.

When our pediatrician heard the news, he decided that the tissue should be sent to a special Army hospital out East for further examination. We nervously and prayerfully waited for an answer.

In the meantime, the confirmation candidates and their parents were invited to a mini-service in the church in preparation for receiving the sacrament. As part of the ceremony, the parents were asked to trace a cross on the forehead of their child. I traced a cross with my finger right over the scar on Tom's head.

The very next day we received our answer. Dr. Perez called to say that the final report showed no cancer and that he should heal without a problem. Tom is now forty-six years old and has just a small scar on his forehead. Thankfully he has never experienced cancer. I have always considered this a miracle—the power of the cross and the Holy Spirit.

fifty-five

The Miracle Event

*But He said, "The things that are impossible
with people are possible with God."*

— Luke 18:27

I WAS A HEALTHY fifty-four-year-old wife and mother until November 1975. I began to have a problem that caused my head and neck to turn to the left. The problem gradually increased. When I walked, read the paper, cooked, cleaned the house, or no matter what I did, my head would move to the left side. I thought it was my eyes, so I saw my eye doctor. He found nothing wrong.

By April 1977, my head would not come back to the center. My head stayed turned toward my left shoulder. I went to my family doctor. I was going through my change and also had bursitis very bad in the left muscle and shoulder. I took some medication for that problem. The doctor said that the head turning was a reaction from the medicine.

I was still getting worse, so my doctor ordered X-rays of my neck and changed my medication. The X-rays indicated degeneration of the neck disc, but he said there was nothing to worry about.

I went to a neurologist in June. He examined me and said that it looked like torticollis. He put me on a muscle relaxant. I wore a collar for five weeks. I took therapy three times a week for four weeks. The therapy consisted of having forty-five pounds of traction pull on my neck for half an hour. I also had X-rays, a CT scan of my neck, and an EEG.

By July I was back at the neurologist's office again. Nothing new showed up on the tests. So, I took off the collar, stopped traction, and continued with my medicine. Then I went to a new neurologist for a second opinion. He stopped all medication and said he agreed with the diagnosis of torticollis.

I went back to my first neurologist. My next treatment was to use hot packs and aspirin as needed.

My first neurologist told me in October that he was very sorry that he could not help me, saying that they don't know what causes this or how to treat it. He said it is very rare. He said they used to operate but found that the patient was worse after the surgery, so they stopped operating. He said I could crawl into a corner, feel sorry for myself and be a vegetable, or make the best of it and do what I could with it. He also said I would have this for the rest of my life.

It was not easy to accept. I felt like a freak. I could not look at anyone when I talked because my head was facing over my left shoulder. It was hard to do anything, but I did my best.

My family was behind me 100 percent. I became very discouraged and depressed for my family. One day I sat down and gave myself a good talking to. I made up my mind that, if I had to live with this, then I would make the best of it. I prayed that the good Lord would let me live long enough so I could lick this—it would not lick me!

I would sit in chairs sideways and stand sideways. It was embarrassing for me when I'd meet new people. People would stare at me when I was in public places. I would turn my body sideways and stand sideways so that I wouldn't look so unnatural. I would do what I could with it. I could not sleep on my right side or back. I was no longer able to drive or do many of the activities I used to do.

I was unable to work at my job at the sewing machine factory, and I was turned down for disability. They said this was not a disability; it was an inconvenience.

After almost nineteen years of living with my head turned to one side, and unable to turn it straight ahead, or to the right, I was pretty much resigned to live my life as best I could. I was in constant pain. It felt like I had a "stiff neck" that never went away. It was important to me to try and make it as convenient as possible for my family. They came first for me, and I didn't want to burden them.

I continued to see my neurologist and began to see a chiropractor too. Over the years I had other problems too. I broke my foot, got shingles on my face, had a breast tumor on my right breast, and cared for my husband until he died of Lou Gehrig's disease.

In August 1994, my daughter, son-in-law, and grandsons invited me along on a family vacation to Disney World in Orlando, Florida. We drove down in their motor home from Oswego, New York, to Florida. I didn't want my family to be hindered by my condition and spoil their vacation. When I agreed to go with them on their vacation, I was determined to make the best of everything.

Then my daughter surprised the life out of me by arranging for me to meet Mickey Mouse at his house. Some people might think it is crazy, but I always loved Mickey. It was such a thrill for me to see him in person! I rapped at the door and he asked me in. I opened my arms and said to him, "Would you give a little old lady a big hug?" He gave me a nice big hug! I was thrilled to death!

But the biggest surprise was yet to come. The next day, on our way back home, I was sitting quietly as usual, looking out the left side of the window as we drove along in the motor home. **Out of the clear blue, it felt like the good Lord put His two hands on my head so gently and moved my head from left to right!** It moved so easily. I was able to control it myself, with no pain and no shaking. What a wonderful feeling! I wanted to shout real loud because I was so happy, but at the same time, I was really scared. I was afraid that maybe it wouldn't last and would freeze to the other side. I called out to my youngest grandson and motioned for him to come back by me—I had something to show him. He was looking at me. I moved my head from left to right on my own power.

He cried with joy, "Nana, you moved your head! I've never seen it turn!" Then he went up front and got his mother to tell her that Nana wanted to see her. The tears were running down my face, but they were tears of joy and excitement, and still I was not sure if what just happened was real or would last.

For me, it truly was a miracle. To this day, *I can still feel those gentle hands on my head*.

I called all of the doctors and explained what happened. They were all very happy for me because they knew that I was living with torticollis for twenty-two years. They called it a miracle! I had no medication except for the aspirin, moist heat, my faith, and determination.

I thank the good Lord for what He's done for me. I thank my family for their understanding and support, as well as the doctors who tried their best to help me. I especially thank Dr. Galvin and Dr. Nickelson, who never gave up on me and took such an interest in my case. I consider myself blessed to have all of their love and so many hugs to go around! I have lived long enough to lick it—it did not lick me. I told Heidi to please tell my story so that others will always have hope!

— *Mary Bernadette Hurley*

Mary Bernadette (Bernie to her friends) has continued to enjoy her life and is very active and independent. She takes care of her own home, including shoveling snow! She has become a strong positive role model and support system for her family, as well as many elderly people who are homebound or ill.

She has never sat home feeling sorry for herself. She continues to travel from the Midwest and up and down the East Coast with family and alone. In the past two years she has taken long car trips every summer to Connecticut, Maine, Massachusetts, has played mini-golf, has ridden a merry-go-round (the horse, not the seat!) and got on and of it by herself at the age of eighty-seven, been on a sailboat, flown to Florida and Chicago by herself, walked daily, spoiled her family baking cookies and pies, and taken senior citizen trips to shows, casinos, and for sightseeing.

Her family is very important to her, and she spends a great deal of time with them. She has seen three generations grow up and delights in the accomplishments of her great-grandson, as well as the many that have adopted her as their "Nana."

fifty-six

Miracles Do Happen

*Trust in the Lord with all your heart and do not lean on your
own understanding. In all your ways acknowledge Him, and He
will make your paths straight. Do not be wise in your own eyes;
fear the Lord and turn away from evil. It will be healing to your
body and refreshment to your bones.*

— Proverbs 3:5-8

MY WIFE, CHRISTIANNA, AND I will never forget the moment we heard the words, "Your child may have water on the brain." The nurse performing our second ultrasound saw something that caused him to ask us to usher our oldest child from the room in order to tell us what he had discovered. That act alone sent our minds racing with worry. After the words were spoken, our minds went numb. Only when we reached our car in the parking lot of the hospital did it hit us. We both held each other and cried. "Water on the brain?" We couldn't even contemplate what that was at the time.

Normally, a second ultrasound is unwarranted. However, my wife's doctor ordered one because, based on her first ultrasound, there was a notation in her file that she might have a placental lake. He said that it was very unlikely that she had any serious issues but, because I was a lawyer and there was a written record indicating the possibility of this condition, however remote, he wasn't about to take any chances. Without the second ultrasound, we would not have discovered our daughter's hydrocephalus for at least six months after birth and until potentially irreversible damage would have occurred to her brain. Catching hydrocephalus before birth through an ultrasound that was almost never given—miracle #1.

During our first visit with specialists following the news of our daughter's condition, we were told that if we so chose we could abort the pregnancy. Nothing in our belief system would allow us to consider for even the slightest moment such an option. We, as well as our baby's grandparents, had both of our First United Methodist churches praying for our daughter, before and after her birth.

However, our belief system would be tested further, as several feelings overwhelmed us. We felt sad, sorry for ourselves, and alone. To overcome those kinds of feelings, we tried to learn as much as we could about hydrocephalus, to be sure we were prepared to take care of a child whose diagnosis before birth was somewhere between severely disabled and relatively normal. Just when we were feeling our worst, we discovered the Hydrocephalus Association. We devoured the information on the association's Web site and immediately decided to become members. The thought that there were others with similar challenges and that we were not alone was uplifting. Finding the association and being part of something important for our daughter's care—miracle #2.

Michaela was born into the loving arms of parents who were well informed and quickly learning to cope with the idea of having a child with challenges. Within three days following her birth, her shunt was inserted.

October of 2006, just before her seventh birthday, Michaela complained of stomach pain. After asking her some questions, we learned that she was feeling tenderness along her shunt tract. Even though we have learned a great deal about hydrocephalus since her birth many years ago, none of the materials we have read has taught us how not to be "nervous Nelly" parents. Exceeding more than one speed limit, we rushed her to the hospital.

Several tests and hours of excruciating pain were endured by Michaela before we learned she had a shunt infection. How is that possible after six years of not having a problem? It was as if all our knowledge of hydrocephalus disappeared and all that was left was that numb feeling we had when we were first told of her condition. Michaela would spend nine days with an external ventricular drain running from the center of her brain into a bag beside her hospital bed. She was scared and confused. We had never told her that she had a shunt. Over the years, we didn't want her to feel different from other children and be worried about something that she couldn't completely understand. After nine days of feeling a tube coming out of the top of her head, she quickly learned that she had a serious condition.

And then it happened. The doctor said words that, again, we will never forget: "She is not draining much fluid, and she may not need the shunt anymore." This time our minds raced not with worry but with dreams of her playing sports, living on her own at college, and raising her own children without the fear of a shunt malfunction. It was almost too good to be true.

After almost seven years of being shunted, Michaela had her shunt removed. We asked every neurosurgical nurse we encountered whether this was common; most responded that they had never seen a child "heal" herself like this. It has been almost six months since the removal, and each follow-up CT scan has given us positive results. The high likelihood of our daughter being shunt free for life—miracle #3.

Ever since Michaela learned to smile and speak to people, she has been the most loving and compassionate child we have ever seen. As naturally biased parents, we started to fully understand the depth of her wonderful spirit when others began noticing it. Several moments come to mind. When Michaela was just a toddler, she flirted with a senior couple several tables away at a local restaurant. She smiled and expressed such a loving spirit, the senior couple remarked while walking by our table on their way out, "Thank you for letting us enjoy your child."

Maybe it was the time she hugged her younger brother during a school musical with tears swelling in her eyes because in her words, "I just love him so much." Or maybe it was the time when she picked a rose from our rose bush in our front yard to give to her older sister, to make her feel better after a fight they had just had. Perhaps it was the time when a grandmother at our church noted that her granddaughter had never spoken many words or felt the desire to be friends with anyone until the day she gave Michaela her favorite stuffed animal and a hug because Michaela had opened her up when no one else could.

Maybe the real miracle is something more subtle. Maybe the real miracle lies within the spirit of a little girl whose love and compassion continuously changes the world around her.

— *H. Richard Hagen*

fifty-seven

Trisha's Lump

The Lord is my light and my salvation; whom shall I fear? The
Lord is the defense of my life; whom shall I dread?

— Psalms 27:1

O NE DAY WHEN MY sixteen-year-old daughter, Trisha, came out
of her daily shower, she asked me to verify something she found
on her breast. As I touched the location she pointed at, my heart
started to pound out of my chest. What I felt was a very hard, large lump.
Panic set in. I asked her if she just discovered this, and she replied, "Eleven
months ago."

With this, I screamed at the top of my lungs, "Oh, my God, help us!" I couldn't
believe she never said anything to me before; apparently she was too embarrassed
and also felt that she was much too young to have anything really wrong with her.

How many times had I told my teenage daughters to examine themselves during
their showers? How many times had I given them the warning signs that might
be harmful to their bodies?

Trisha just looked at me in horror, only to see the horror in my eyes reflect back
to hers. She just broke down in hysteria.

I screamed to my husband, who was somewhere else in the house. As he
came up the stairs, I ran to the phone to call the gynecologist. She returned my

desperate call and told me to take Trisha into the office the following morning for an examination.

As I put down the telephone, I told my husband that we should pray over our daughter. We have been **born-again** Christians since the early seventies, and my husband has received the gift of tongues. I also believe he has the gift of healing. We all prayed, but I have to say that was one of the longest nights of my life.

Trying to give it all to Jesus, I prayed unceasingly. I took Trisha to the doctor first thing in the morning.

After the examination, the doctor told me that she definitely had a lump that needed serious attention. She took some ultrasounds of the lump. She gave us the name of a surgeon to see, for a biopsy, and told us that the biopsy, in itself, might leave some horrific scarring, as the lump was so big.

I tried to remain calm for my daughter's sake, as she sobbed tear after tear. I was terrified, but then thought that I was not trusting in the Lord, as I always preached to others. The Lord wanted me to trust in Him. He wanted us to trust in Him. As I remembered that, my fears calmed.

When we returned home, I put in a call to my father, who is a physician and also a Christian. He said they would put Trisha on their church's prayer chain. I also called the rest of my family, who also would pray for her.

My friends were also very supportive, by having prayers said for Trisha at their churches too. Of course, all these requests that we made to them had to be in secret because Trisha was so embarrassed over her condition. I suppose teenagers have some peculiar ways of thinking.

The appointment was made with the surgeon, but we had to wait another two weeks, the hardest two weeks ever. In the meantime, we went to see my cousin, a chiropractor, for help. He is also a Christian. We prayed over Trisha in his office. Then he gave us some vitamin supplements and a diet for her to follow. We went home, tried to remain calm, and put our faith in the Lord.

Every evening my husband and I prayed over Trisha asking for God's help. We stood on each side of her, with the palms of our hands facing her body, during the prayers. We prayed every evening for two weeks, during which time she was extremely nervous. My husband and I prayed over her once again, asking for her healing. It was the day before New Year's Eve.

Of course, being human, I was expecting the worst, even though I prayed over and over again. Because my faith was wavering, I was having a difficult time letting God take complete control of the situation. When will I ever learn?

The nurse called Trisha into the inner office. We all took a deep breath. Moments later, the doctor came out with our daughter and exclaimed, "Happy New Year! I don't know why you came in to see me, because she has nothing there now. I would not have believed there was a lump if I didn't see the ultrasound."

We all three just looked at each other with such a sigh of relief. This was truly a miracle. God comes to our rescue. Whom shall we fear?

So far, there has been no sign of any returning tumors. That was twelve years ago. Praise God!

— *Lenore M. Kelly*

fifty-eight

Miracle on the Hill

I will give thanks to the Lord with all my heart;
I will tell of all Your wonders. I will be glad and exult
in You; I will sing praise to Your name, O Most High.

— Psalms 9:1-2

THE EXCERPT BELOW COMES from a speech I wrote the beginning of my senior year of high school. I was a student leader for our Kairos retreat. At the time Kairos was a four-day retreat that was led by both senior high school students who had previously made the retreat and a few faculty members from the high school. The retreat focused mostly on helping the junior or senior high school student find and/or develop his or her own personal relationship with God. Each student leader was assigned a particular topic (e.g., love in action, leaders) and was responsible for speaking to his or her peers on that topic. My topic was "study," which was supposed to demonstrate my experience in finding ways to know God. Part of my speech revolved around the miracles in Medjugorje that I witnessed and experienced with my family the summer before my junior year in high school. The excerpt below reads as I wrote it over twenty years ago. While I like to think my writing ability has definitely improved with age and experience, I think the raw, uncut version below provides a gullible, honest, and undiluted account of faith in God, family, and oneself, told from a teenager's point of view. My trip to Medjugorje made a momentous impact on my life. Although I was raised by my parents to believe in God, attended Mass, and was a student in a Catholic high school, I believed because I was told to believe. Prior to my trip, I do not think I really had a "relationship" with God, and definitely never truly questioned my faith. The trip to Medjugorje provided me with a true personal connection with God and made me see that it was okay to question, without diluting, my faith. I was blessed and fortunate enough to have an experience in my life where I actually saw and felt the presence of God. That blessing continues to keep me rooted in my faith today.

During my sophomore year, in high school, my mom took a trip with my grandma to Medjugorje. My mom knew nothing about where she was going, except that she was going to Yugoslavia. About two days before she left, she checked out some articles on Medjugorje for a little background information. The only reason my mom was excited was that this was going to be her first trip to Europe. I knew when she came back that Medjugorje had changed her. Usually, after trips my mother has taken, she would come home and go to sleep. After arriving home from this trip, my mom couldn't stop talking about this "miracle of Mary" place.

She told us about the "miracle of Mary" place—that she witnessed the miracle of the sun. The sun, she said, appeared to her as a bright fiery collage of dancing colors. I believed my mom, without a doubt, because I knew she wouldn't lie to me about anything. Another thing my mom had never done before, was ask us to say the rosary together as a family. She told us that one of Mary's messages was to pray as a family.

Her experience did not wear out, either. There were times we all thought she was a bit crazy. She would hold her rosary out and claim that there were gold specks on it. She was so fascinated by her experience that she gathered up as much information as possible. I never in my life had seen my mom so full of energy and acceptance of a situation.

The next month, May, she asked each one in our family if we would like to go to Medjugorje in August. I went merely because of my fascination with what occurred to my mom, my endless curiosity, and because, like my other two sisters, I wanted to see Europe. So, in August we left for Medjugorje. That is when my inner journey to God began. This is when my study of God became my path of life.

What I felt and what I saw in Medjugorje that summer changed my life forever. I witnessed several miracles that proved to me God was real. My family and I were there during the Assumption, August 15. That night, Mary was to appear, dressed in gold, to the visionaries on a hill, where she had shown herself the first time to them. The city that night was very crowded, and so was the hill where she was to appear. A group of us, including my family, walked out to where we could see the hill. Just before Mary was to appear, someone pointed out a star in the sky. It was the only gold star in the sky. People were yelling, screaming, and crying. I couldn't understand why I thought some people were either going crazy or just faking it. Then I heard someone say "Oh, my God, it's making the sign of the cross!" I looked but saw nothing. I felt so disappointed. I only saw the gold star. I felt God did not want me to see this, but my mom apparently did. She borrowed somebody's binoculars so I could see what everyone else saw with their naked eyes.

At first, I thought I was moving my arms as I was looking. I asked my mom if I was moving my arms, and then I asked her to keep my hands steady. She told me they weren't moving. I felt so special at that moment. I was chosen by God to see this star make the sign of the cross over and over again. I started to cry at that moment. I cried because of all the doubt and anxiety I had built up because I thought God didn't want me involved in this miracle. I also felt guilty at even thinking that. However, the feeling of love I received through that star made up for all my past uncertainties.

Right after viewing the sign of the cross miracle, someone pointed to the hill where Mary was to appear and the star was forgotten. Because it was nighttime, everyone on the hill carried flashlights. There were other lights in the city, but for the next fifteen minutes the only lights seen were those on the hill. The flashlights held by the people on the mountain formed the crucifix. I could see Jesus' head hanging, His knees bent, and I could see the crucifix!! I felt so special, so overwhelmingly happy to think that God was allowing me to see this miracle. After the crucifix, another image appeared. It was a cross. I clearly felt God's presence beside me, all around me. I was crying again by this time; I could not get over the feeling that this was actually happening to me. I was waiting to wake up from a dream.

Five minutes later, the cross faded out and the profile of Jesus with the crown of thorns was in sight. I felt really guilty at seeing the crown of thorns. I remembered all of what Jesus went through for us, and I had given nothing in return to Him. I felt how selfish I had been in not giving God any time in my life.

Soon, following this miracle a dove appeared. I felt an inner peace. I knew God forgave me for not giving Him more time. The next image was in gold. The feeling I had was unexplainable. My emotions were full speed, and my tears never stopped falling. This was the proof I had been looking for. I encountered God everywhere. I found God through this experience. I was fortunate to find my God this way.

While in Medjugorje, I prayed for a miracle for myself, to be rid of some ugly and sometimes painful plantar warts. From about the time I was in fifth grade, I developed horrible plantar warts on my left heel. This seemed to be caused from all my swimming and sports. Over the years, I had seen several doctors to remove these warts. I made two attempts to burn the warts with medicine, had surgery, and laser removal. I tried everything.

During our flight home, I experienced another miracle. For some reason, and now I cannot recall why, I took off my shoes. I was more than elated and amazed to find that the plantar warts had disappeared; all that was left on my heel was the scar tissue from the many years of trying to "heal" myself! God answered my prayer!

• fifty-nine •

Mysterious Medical Miracle

*O Lord, You have searched me and known me. You know when
I sit down and when I rise up; You understand my thought
from afar. You scrutinize my path and my lying down, and are
intimately acquainted with all my ways. Even before there is a
word on my tongue, behold, O Lord, You know it all. You have
enclosed me behind and before, and laid Your hand upon me. Such
knowledge is too wonderful for me; it is too high, I cannot attain
to it. Where can I go from your Spirit?*

— Psalms 139:1-7

O N SEPTEMBER 12, 2008, my daughter Maddie had what I thought was a stomach bug. She complained of pain in her stomach in the area of her belly button. She stayed home from school that day. Throughout the day, she had a fever. She also began complaining of pain in her "pit" and pointed to her right armpit.

The next day, September 13, was poor Maddie's fifth birthday. She could hardly sit up. Her fever was high. She complained of pain in her back. I took her to the doctor. They diagnosed her with pneumonia. She had a high white blood cell count. I was told her X-ray looked pretty bad. Maddie's doctor decided she needed to be admitted to the hospital.

Many people prayed with and for Maddie while she was there. She was able to come home after three days.

Several days later, the doctor wanted to check Maddie's progress. He ordered another X-ray to be taken. While we waited for the results, I noticed a crowd forming in the hallway. Several nurses and the doctor were looking at the X-ray. The radiologist asked me if I had possibly stepped into the X-ray while it was being performed, because there was something she didn't understand in the picture. After I answered no, she called me and Maddie into the hall and showed us a hand, which was clearly placed over the affected area on Maddie's chest. She pointed out two things: first, the hand was larger than her hand, so it couldn't be that she had somehow touched the X-ray, causing the image, and, secondly, there were no bones in the hand.

Maddie told us that when she was in the hospital, Jesus touched her and made her feel better, although it took about one month for Maddie to regain her strength. I guess there are other ways this hand could have been transferred to the X-ray, but we choose to believe that Maddie's answer is the most logical!

To view Maddie's chest X-ray go to:

www.touchedbythegraceofGod.com

www.facebook.com (Enter *Touched by the Grace of God* in the search window.)

Prayers That Were Answered

sixty

Moment With Jesus

You will seek Me and find Me when you
search for me with all your heart.

— Jeremiah 29:13

I
N AUGUST OF 2004, I had the most meaningful and tender encounter with Jesus. I would love to share this experience with you.

In 2002, I was diagnosed with breast cancer and went through chemo and radiation. All was going well, until August of 2004. At that time, two more spots of concern were found in the area of my affected breast. I had to have two more biopsies. These biopsies were done on a Friday. I tried not to dwell on this over the weekend. I was blessed with strength to do this.

On the following Tuesday, I knew the results would be available. I was at work that day. I placed a call to my doctor for the results. I was awaiting a return call. I went to our lounge area to take a coffee break. As I sat there, I was praying that Jesus would be with me, no matter what the results were. I prayed for comfort and peace. At that time, *I felt His arms around me*! It was an awesome feeling. I felt completely at peace and was able to give up my worrying to Him.

Although this only lasted a few seconds, it has made a definite change in my life. I know now that no matter what I am experiencing or feeling, I am not doing it alone. Jesus is with me all the way. What else could I possibly need?

I am extremely grateful for that experience and also for the results of my biopsies, which were negative . . . **praise God**!

—Anne Pauly

• sixty-one •

A Tender Calling

Oh give thanks to the Lord, call upon His name; make known His deeds among the peoples. Sing to Him, sing praises to Him; speak of all His wonders. Glory in His holy name; let the heart of those who seek the Lord be glad.

— Psalms 105:1-3

WHEN I BEGAN WORKING at my parish's elementary/middle school as a mental health counselor, I understood that, for professional reasons, I and my family would need to find another parish to attend. Although the task of finding a new spiritual home was not eagerly embraced, its practical necessity was logically accepted. After all, we had come to be quite comfortable in the parish community after nine years. This was where my own two children had spent a substantial portion of their childhoods, received the sacraments, and attended school. Yet, the area in which we lived included a large Catholic population with numerous parish communities in neighboring cities, so the prospect of finding another suitable church seemed simple enough. "Seemed" is the operative word here. We looked, we visited, and we revisited, and looked again. For one reason or another, we just didn't seem to feel comfortable, "at home," in any of the parish communities. We finally settled on attending a nearby church, hoping that with time we would feel part of the community life.

However, after almost two years had passed, we still felt our home was elsewhere. But where? And why? What was it within us that we kept yearning for? We didn't know. Yet, we did know that when we found it, we'd know it. Perhaps it was the sense that, yes, this is where we belong. What a powerful human need that is for all of us—we all want to belong somewhere and, more importantly, to someone. One day, I shared my thoughts and feelings about these frustrations with a humble and holy woman. She worked as the Director of Liturgy at our former parish and also helped guide me spiritually from time to time. She suggested a parish we hadn't considered and encouraged us to pray for guidance with confidence that an answer would most assuredly come.

My sights were set on the next Sunday, and my heart on another chance to find a new home. I realized how important this really was to me, and I prayed fervently for increased trust in God's providence. Now, it happened that the week before we would attend Mass at the newly suggested parish, I saw on television the movie *Trip to Bountiful* starring Geraldine Page. Her performance earned her an academy award for best actress, and, if you've never seen this film, you have missed a cinematic gem. It's a moving story with an incredibly beautiful theme song titled, "Softly, Tenderly, Jesus Is Calling." I had never seen the movie before nor heard its soundtrack. All week long, I thought about the movie's story line and hummed and sang its theme song. I even ordered a copy of the film for myself. I discussed the movie with family and friends, and more than likely drove everyone nuts with my enthusiasm about it.

Sunday soon arrived, and off we went to attend Mass at the "new" parish. My husband and I arrived early, so we could look around a bit and spend some time praying before Mass began. I was kneeling with my eyes fixed on the body of Jesus hung on a large, black, wooden cross behind the altar. The sculpted body was so life-like it seemed as if Jesus was actually there before us suffering His final agony. I closed my eyes and began to pray with all my heart for the Lord's guidance. I asked that, if this was the church for us, He would somehow show us, give us a sign, something, anything to let us know this was where He wanted us to worship Him and belong in community. As I continued to pray in silence, absorbed in my own inner thoughts, I very slowly and gently became faintly aware of a lovely song the music minister was playing on the piano. It sounded so familiar, yet I knew I'd never heard it in church before. It was on the tip of my tongue, so to speak. I began to pay closer attention to the melody and stopped my prayer when the sudden realization hit me like a physical force and I knew!

It was the theme song from the movie *Trip to Bountiful*! I swung around to tell my husband sitting in the pew and, straining to keep from shouting, I cried, "That's the song from the movie!" My heart was pounding.

He responded, "It can't be."

I excitedly whispered once again, "It is, it is! It's the song from *Trip to Bountiful*"! I saw his jaw drop, and he mumbled something about it being unbelievable. But it was believable, and I quickly threw open the hymnal before me, searching for the song and its words. I wanted to read every word. Sure enough, I found it and I knew without a doubt that we had found our spiritual home.

The song and the lyrics I read were, I believe, an answer to prayer and no mere coincidence. I had never heard that song played in church before or since this experience. But, I do believe the Lord used it to help us know His will for us and His unfailing providence. We joined the parish following this and have already reaped much fruit from our membership there. May you be blessed as you realize that it's no coincidence you have now shared in our encounter with the Lord. May God bless you all!

— *Marcia Rau*

sixty-two

Morning Prayer Miracle

The Lord your God is in your midst, a victorious warrior. He
will exult over you with joy; He will be quiet in His love, He
will rejoice over you with shouts of joy.

— Zephaniah 3:17

O NE THURSDAY MORNING IN February 2002, I was scheduled to lead
Morning Prayer at my church. Morning Prayer begins at 8:30 a.m.; at
8:25 a.m. I was by myself in the chapel, so I began to pray to the Lord
to bring one person to join me for prayer. A few minutes later, a woman came in,
expecting Mass to begin. I invited her to join me in Morning Prayer and briefly
explained the format for Morning Prayer.

Shortly after we began to pray, I could see she was upset about something. When
we came to the "petitions," I prayed for the teenage grandson of a homebound
parishioner I visit on a monthly basis. I prayed for the Lord's guidance for his
doctor, for proper diagnosis, and for treatment for his continued vomiting.
Immediately after we finished with Morning Prayer, the woman asked me for
the name and phone number of the parents of the teenage boy who was vomiting
because her son was also vomiting, and she was so worried and beside herself she
didn't think she could take another day!

I told her I was a Minister of Care and could not give out personal information
without approval, because of confidentiality rules, but I would be more than happy

to take her name and phone number and pass it along to the family if she would like. She thanked me and we prayed once more. Then we both left the chapel.

Days later, I was able to talk with her again and found out that not only did the other family contact her, but they also invited her family to come over to their home.

Within a few days, they began to see an improvement in their son—the first in several months! She also shared with me that she had no intention of coming to church that morning. She was actually on her way to work that morning but didn't feel she could handle it. The next thing she knew, she was parked in the church parking lot and entering the church!

I truly believe this was a miracle from God for several reasons. First of all, I only lead Morning Prayer two Thursdays out of the month, and this woman came on one of the Thursdays I was there. Secondly, that particular morning no one else came to Morning Prayer, so there was the opportunity to share with total privacy. Thirdly, if I had not been a Minister of Care, I would never have prayed for the boy who was ill, and the fact that I actually used the word "vomit" in my prayer petition is what "triggered" this mom to ask me about this family!

I thank God for the opportunity to be used by Him to bring these two families together to help and support each other through this very difficult time. God has been and continues to be glorified!

sixty-three

Peace at the End of the Rainbow

*God said, "This is the sign of the covenant which I am making
between Me and you and every living creature that is with you,
for all successive generations; I set My bow in the cloud, and it
shall be for a sign of a covenant between Me and the earth."*

— Genesis 9:12-13

MY FATHER HAD NASOPHARYNGEAL cancer, which is cancer behind the sinus. We were told that usually a person suffocates to death as the tumor grows into the throat area. The cancer later was in remission. However, on June 7, 2006, we found out that my dad's cancer was back and probably never completely went away.

I went to church every Sunday in Wheeling, Illinois, and prayed, "Please don't make my dad suffer." One night after June 7, I am not completely sure of the date, I had a dream. In the dream I was selected to appear in a magazine advertisement for one of my company's products (at the time, I was working in the food industry). I was in a room with seven colleagues. One person was in charge of setting up the scene, directing us, and telling us where each of us would sit, etc.

I remember walking to a window and looking out at the sky. Then a door opened to a room, and in walked the late Pope John Paul II with an aide. The Pope spoke and said, "I am looking for Christine Hardenburg. I understand that someone very close to you is very ill and is dying."

I said, "Yes, my father is seventy-three, has cancer, has been given little time to live, and I don't want him to suffer."

He replied, "Your father will suffer, as we all will suffer in our own time. Jesus suffered, I suffered with my illness, and you too will suffer someday." I tried interjecting when he said, "To be forty-three, have a young family and to be dying of cancer is difficult."

I kept saying/yelling, "No, no, my father is seventy-three and has cancer."

Pope John Paul II kept saying, "Yes, to be fourty-three, have a young family and to be dying of cancer is difficult."

My dream ended with him walking out of the room and me saying to myself, "What doesn't he get?" I have since interpreted that dream to mean that suffering is a part of life and death and that I should be thankful that I had my dad for as many years as I did, because someone else might not be so lucky.

On Friday, July 28, they told the family that my dad had sepsis (blood poisoning), which come to think of it the late Pope John Paul II also had. The best we could do was put Dad on hospice. Ironically, I had planned a girls' weekend out. We were meeting in St. Charles, Illinois. I was torn; what should I do? My mom told me I should go on the trip to St. Charles and enjoy the time. I decided to go to Angel Kisses, but I cut the trip short and also went to Indiana that Sunday to see my father. The bottom line was that I made it a point to go to Angel Kisses of St. Charles because I knew it would be a place where I could find comfort, based on the stories I had heard from Heidi. I went to the store and loved it. I briefly mentioned my dad's condition to the owner of the shop. She encouraged me to pray at the Mary statue. I felt so at peace.

On Wednesday, August 2, I got the call that I should come back to Indiana as Dad was showing clear signs that the end was near. Due to an unpleasant work situation, I did not leave Wheeling until 7 p.m. I was comforted during the two and a half hour drive as I listened to Relevant Radio. They were praying the rosary. I arrived at my parents' home ten minutes before the priest did, which I was very thankful for because my dad was still coherent. I could talk to my dad. I know he could hear and understand me.

On Thursday, my dad had a good day. There didn't seem to be much change.

They had set up my dad's bed in the living room. We would put the television on for him to listen to the ball game, news, etc.

My husband Alan and son Nathan did not make the trip to Indiana because Nathan is only two and a half years old. Every night before Nathan goes to bed he says, "Now I lay me down to sleep . . .." That night I was saying prayers with Nathan over the phone while I was in the same room as my dad.

Sometime after midnight (when I fell asleep), and before 4:45 a.m. (when I woke up), my dad passed away. Why I woke up at 4:45 a.m., I have no idea. I slept on the couch both nights so I could be there in case Dad passed away. As soon as I woke up, I knew my dad passed away. When I told my sister JoAnn, she said that she had been dreaming about Dad. She said that Dad was pounding his fist into his hand. She was disturbed by it enough to wake up and notice that the time was 4:30 a.m. The day my dad passed away was also my mom's birthday (August 4).

My entire family decided that we would meet on Dad's birthday at the cemetery in Merrillville, Indiana. (His birthday was September 30.) Unfortunately, my mom was in the hospital that weekend with congestive heart failure complications.

Alan, Nathan, and I went on our own time. We left Wheeling around 11:30 a.m. and drove to Merrillville. The day was beautiful. The sun was bright, not a cloud in the sky. It was warm enough to wear shorts. We decided to eat lunch before going to the cemetery. As we were finishing lunch, the storm clouds were rolling in, and, as we made our way to the cemetery, there was thunder and lightning. I did not want to get out of the car because my dad is buried under a tree. So we drove around looking for my grandparents' graves before stopping back at my dad's site. Finally, the rain let up, but not completely, and, since there was no longer thunder and lightning, we decided to get out of the car. Naturally, I was upset. I was crying and praying. I kept asking Dad, "Are you okay? Are you in heaven?" Then suddenly behind me the sun peeked out of a cloud. When I looked up in front of me, a double rainbow was in the sky! At that point, I knew that my dad was speaking to me saying that he is okay!

We went back to the cemetery on Veterans Day, with my brother and mother, to help pick out my father's marker. From the time I awoke, it was raining (no thunderstorms, just drizzling). After we left the cemetery we all went to lunch. When we were on I-65 heading back to Illinois, a rainbow appeared in the sky!

As a side note, when I was a senior in high school, my family went on a trip to Colorado. It was Dad's favorite vacation spot. We also went to Cheyenne, Wyoming, on that trip. If you have never been there, it is gorgeous. Believe it or not, there is a zoo on Cheyenne Mountain. So, one afternoon, my dad took us there. We were walking to the zoo. My father called me to his side. What we could see was that where we were on the mountain it was sunny, but below it was raining and storming. While looking down, we could see a rainbow.

I took many pictures. For the longest time I had that picture hanging in my room at college. Unfortunately, I don't know what I did with it. I had forgotten that story until almost three months after we went to the cemetery in September. I know that my father is giving me a sign through the rainbows, just like our Heavenly Father uses rainbows as a sign of His promise to us.

— *Christine A. Hardenburg*

sixty-four

"Mary, Help Me!"

"He will call upon Me, and I will answer him; I will be with him in trouble; I will rescue him and honor him.

— Psalms 91:15

IN THE FALL OF 2004, I was very sick. I had a number of problems, all occurring simultaneously. After three visits, in six days, to the emergency room at Northwest Community Hospital, it was obvious that further testing needed to be done.

One of the first specialists I saw was a cardiologist. My stress test and EKG's all were normal. I still had heart pain. My cardiologist didn't feel that my heart was the problem. He said that he would perform an angiogram to help me rule out my heart as the source of my problem, so I could move on.

The night before the angiogram I prayed to Mary. I said, "Mary, you have to help me get through this. I need to see light through the tunnel."

In the morning I prayed again. "Mary, please help me through this," I said.

The first thing I did at the hospital was check in with my insurance card. I noticed that the receptionist entering the information into the computer was named Mary.

Next, a nurse told me to change into two gowns and lie on the bed. When I read her name tag, it said Mary.

A young male nurse came into the room to take me to another room for preparation for the procedure. As he pushed me through the halls he asked me, "How are you doing?"

I said, "I am scared."

Then the male nurse told me, "Most people wouldn't admit that. Don't worry; we will take good care of you. You have a good doctor."

In the next room, some more people came in to put some IV's in my arm. Then I had to change exam beds. When I changed beds, I accidentally pulled out one of my IV's and blood squirted all over.

Then another nurse came into the room. When she saw what happened, she told her co-workers, "This is how you do it." Then she told me, "Don't worry. I will be taking very good care of you." I looked at her name tag. Her name was Mary.

My angiogram procedure went well; I only had ten percent blockage. The good news was that my heart was fine, and Mary did help me!

sixty-five

Caring for Mom

*Honor your father and your mother, that your days may be
prolonged in the land which the Lord your God gives you.*

— Exodus 20:12

M Y STORY BEGINS WHEN my eighty-five-year-old mother, who was living alone, slipped outside and fell on the ice near the garage door of her home. She fractured her humerus, the large bone in the upper arm running from the shoulder to the elbow. None of her adult children were home at the time. She struggled to get back into the house, and finally she managed to call a close neighbor who drove her to the hospital.

During the course of Mother's recovery, she was able to be at home with our help. I assisted on weekends. My brother stayed with her for days at a time, and my sister visited whenever she could. After three weeks, the changing weather of late fall began to take its toll on Mother's arthritic back and right leg. She struggled to walk or even turn over in bed. We knew that she needed to go for rehab at our local nursing home. After a few weeks there, she got stronger, and was able to walk the halls of the nursing home, as her fractured arm healed. At the end of a month, she was able to go home. But now we faced another problem about her care, and this is where the "Angel Story" begins.

We needed to find viable home health care in our small community. I began to contact social services in Rockford, Sterling, and Dekalb, Illinois. Availability was an issue. We really didn't know any of these people, and the cost was high. We were fearful that we would not be able to find appropriate help to care for Mother.

A few weeks after Mother came home from her rehab at the nursing home, my brother came to town for a few days to take care of the taxes on her house. He went to the bank in Rochelle, filled out a form, had it notarized at the bank, and drove to Oregon, Illinois, the county seat for Ogle County, to record the document. Once he got there and approached the appropriate county window, he was told that the bank in Rochelle had not notarized the document. Now he had to return to Rochelle, go back to the bank, and seek out another person at the bank.

The person he found at the bank turned out to be a high school classmate of mine, Roxanne. My brother knew her too. She asked him why he was in Rochelle. Then he explained about our mother's situation: from her fall, to rehab, and home again, and that he was in town to take care of her taxes.

He also told her that we were looking for someone to take care of Mother for a few hours in the morning. Roxanne said she knew a woman who cared for the elderly. She was the sister of another high school friend of mine. Roxanne gave him a phone number. We made some calls and found our angel named Doris. Doris agreed to work for our family two or three hours a day, five days a week, at a very affordable price, even though her evenings were spent caring for another woman (another classmate's elderly mother).

What are the chances of this ever happening? I had been praying for assistance, for guidance, to somehow find help for our mother, and along came Doris. If my brother had not needed to return to the bank to have the paper notarized a second time, it is not very likely that we would have made the connection with Roxanne, and we never would have known about or employed Doris.

For over a year, Doris helped Mother a few hours each day. She brought groceries, did the laundry, and would drive Mother to her appointments, since she could no longer drive. Even though Mother's mind was not good, she looked forward to daily visits with Doris.

As a family we have been blessed that the Lord sent us an angel to guide us through this difficult situation. My dear mother passed away on August 11, 2009, after living a year in a nursing facility where 24-hour care was needed based on her Alzheimer's/dementia disease. We know that she is at peace and with the Lord.

sixty-six

Our Miracle Baby Jack

"Therefore I will say to you, all things for which
you pray and ask, believe that you have received
them, and they will be granted you."

— Mark 11:24

M Y DAUGHTER'S FIRST PREGNANCY resulted in a miscarriage. Two years later she did deliver a healthy baby boy. After two years, she wanted a little brother or sister for her little boy. She had three miscarriages. It seemed she could get pregnant, but, after six weeks, she would lose the baby. She was extremely depressed.

She and her husband decided to see a specialist. She did get pregnant and had to see the doctor every two or three days for hormone injections. This resulted in headaches that were so severe she could not lift her head off the pillow.

The first trimester went by. After the first ultrasound, she was told there was a problem with the baby's intestines. She was advised to have amniocentesis. After consulting with her regular obstetrician, she was told the test could be harmful to the baby. She and her husband decided not to have the test.

Instead, she would have an ultrasound every week to monitor the baby. In the seventh month she lost her amniotic fluid and had to have bed rest, lying on her right side.

My husband and I are members of a Bible study group. Everyone in the group, and all of our friends, prayed for her and the baby. Two in the group were doctors, and they kept encouraging her. Other doctors told her the baby would have severe problems and never have a normal life. We all just kept praying.

Finally, her OB doctor decided to induce her two weeks early. He felt she was healthy and the baby had a good chance. After two days in labor, she delivered a beautiful baby boy. He was and is perfect.

On October 2, he will be fifteen years old. He is a beautiful, intelligent little boy. We all thank God for him every day. He is our miracle.

— Mary E. Jurewicz

sixty-seven

February 14, 2008

*Jesus answered and said to her, "Everyone who drinks of this
water will thirst again; but whoever drinks of the water that I
will give him shall never thirst; but the water that I will give him
will become in him a well of water springing up to eternal life."*

— John 4:13-14

"EVERYONE WHO DRINKS THIS water will thirst again; but whoever drinks the water I shall give will never thirst." I am sure that most of us have heard this Gospel many times in the past. Maybe we have a hard time distinguishing between the two types of water. Maybe we have a hard time understanding just what is this living water that Jesus talks about. But for me, I recently received a real-life example of just what the difference is, and I will never be the same.

Let me take you back to Valentine's Day 2008. My wife Sharon and I talked about not exchanging gifts. You know that conversation that begins by saying, "Now, do you promise that you aren't getting me anything? Because I am not getting you anything!" And you live up to that until the morning of Valentine's Day, when you ask yourself, "Are you crazy? They always say don't get me anything, and then if you don't, be ready to spend a lot of quality time with the dog!"

So, I finally came to my senses and ran to the only place that was open before work. I found some pants that I thought that she would like. All the pants on the rack were sizes that were not Sharon's size. Then a panic set in and I thought, man, am I going to be in trouble! Suddenly, as if a pair floated down from the sky, the right size appeared—Thank you, God!

The morning went on. We had been in a series of lengthy discussions with our major customer as to when the launch of a new product line was to take place. Having the right amount of inventory on hand to meet the beginning stages of the program was critical, but it was very dependent on the start-up date. We finally got the news that morning. The date was when we had hoped for it to be, and all was good. In fact, I remember saying to myself what a great day this was turning out to be. My temporary thirst was quenched all day by these gifts of water.

Let's fast forward to 3:20 in the afternoon. My cell phone rang. It was my daughter Tracy, who was calling me from college at Northern Illinois University. "Dad," her shaking voice said, "There is a shooting that is taking place here right now. I am in my dorm room, but I am scared."

My mind was racing, but, on the other hand, everything seemed to be in slow motion. Fortunately, she was with her boyfriend Mark, who had come to take her to dinner for Valentine's Day. We talked about them locking the door in the room, closing the curtains, and keeping in contact with us. As a result of the news spreading so quickly, the cell phone system became so busy that this would be the last time that we would talk to Tracy for almost forty-five minutes. That afternoon felt like the equivalent of an eternity.

I quickly turned to the news, which was just breaking. Was there one shooter or two? Where was the shooting taking place? Did the killer escape? How close was all of this activity to where Tracy and Mark were? Over the next hour, the situation started to become a little more clear. The location where the shooting occurred was a few blocks from where Tracy was. She walked right by that room twenty minutes before the shooting. The class that the massacre took place in, was going to be the exact class that Tracy was to be in—that is, if she didn't make a last-minute change in her schedule before the semester had begun. We were relieved to find out that indeed Tracy and Mark were safe, but five of her other classmates were not so fortunate. They had lost their lives to this senseless tragedy. I came to see the gifts of living water that were right in front of me. What were they?

The gift of family became so clear in our eyes. Our family had the gift of life that remained in Tracy and Mark. We had the opportunity to hug and kiss our daughter a few hours thereafter. We had the chance to dry each other's tears as the shock wore off. The realization hit us of how close we had been to losing the most precious gift that we had.

There were her brothers, who a few days ago were arguing with her about whether or not she took the charger to the laptop, writing messages on Facebook, telling all that would read this that they had spent their time afterwards in tears, fearing that their life would never be the same if she was harmed, and that they loved her dearly. There was the gift of friends, calling and e-mailing Sharon and me, offering prayers and support.

There was the gift of faith. This gift was driven home to me while watching the 9 p.m. news that night. The reporter was interviewing a girl who was attending a memorial service at Northern that night. When the reporter asked her why she was at church, she looked up with tear-drenched eyes and said, "There is no answer as to why this happened. All that we can do is to come back to God and put the future in His hands, knowing that we never walk alone."

The next morning, at the Friday 6:45 a.m. Mass, tears flowed from my eyes while looking up at that cross. *I heard Him say to me, "Take my hand. We will walk through this."* That was the best example of living water that I had ever experienced.

The gift of the right size pants and the great news from a customer were great occurrences while they happened, but they were temporary things. They were incidents that will be long forgotten in a few days. They would not quench a thirst for any long period of time.

But the gifts of life, family, friends, and faith were the gifts that would get us through this. These are gifts that, if we choose to cherish them, will quench our thirst forever. So, maybe during these remaining weeks of Lent, instead of chasing those temporary ways to quench our thirst, we can instead look to those gifts which God gives us that remain forever. Those gifts that truly matter are the gifts of life and faith.

Maybe we can begin the process by doing a couple of things. First, look up to His cross and recommit ourselves to walk with the Lord in good times and in bad, not choosing to walk by ourselves. He is waiting to take our hand. And secondly, the first chance that we get, go home and hug our loved ones as hard as we can, telling them what they mean to us. Our tomorrows are never promised to us. It is time that we cherish those real gifts of living water.

—*Jim Gaughan*

• sixty-eight •

Nothing Is Lost

*Or what woman, if she has ten silver coins and loses one coin, does
not light a lamp and sweep the house and search carefully until
she finds it? When she has found it, she calls together her friends
and neighbors, saying, "Rejoice with me, for I have found the coin
which I had lost!" In the same way, I tell you, there is joy in the
presence of the angels of God over one sinner who repents."*

— Luke 15:8-10

YEARS AGO A FRIEND was helping me look for something I had lost. She mentioned to me that I should ask God for help in finding what was lost. She said that she repeated to herself, "Nothing is lost in the kingdom of God" and, sure enough, in time she found what she was looking for.

I used her idea frequently. I really began to see how God would help, even with the smallest request. My husband and two daughters really didn't understand my belief in God's help in finding the lost. I continued to ask for His assistance, and I was able to find my lost "treasures" in God's kingdom.

During a move from one house to another, I lost the stone from a necklace. I began to look everywhere, and of course, I was thinking, "Nothing is lost in the kingdom of God." My girls mentioned to me that my positive thoughts about "Nothing is lost" did not seem to be working.

In time, after about one month, I began to realize that my special stone was in "God's kingdom," just not in my possession. I prayed for peace over my lost treasure, and once in a while I would think, "Nothing is lost."

Six weeks after I lost the stone, my husband and I went to a church dinner. Upon arriving home we found an envelope on the kitchen table. It read, "Nothing is lost in the kingdom of God," and inside I found my lost stone. My daughters had left the envelope on the kitchen table, explaining that they had found the stone at the front door threshold.

We had all walked in and out of that door many times over the previous six weeks and did not see the stone (Our daughters hosted a party for about sixty people that weekend.). Amazingly, the stone was in perfect condition. I am very grateful that God kept the stone safe in His glorious kingdom. My husband and daughters don't tease me about God helping me anymore. God does work in very mysterious ways!

— *Ginger Mueller*

sixty-nine

Out of Gas: Renewed in Faith

*The angel of the Lord encamps around those
who fear Him, and rescues them.*

— Psalms 34:7

O N A VERY HOT day in June, a friend and I decided to drive north in Florida to visit a good buddy of hers, whom she had not seen for some time. She needed to talk to her friend about whether or not she should go back to her controlling husband. We also took her old, small, white dog along for the trip.

We met her friend. Then the three of us took a leisurely drive along the coast of Florida and visited St. Augustine. We had a nice sightseeing trip through the oldest city in Florida and discussed what she should do. We said our goodbyes and drove slowly back to our homes on the west coast of Florida.

On our drive back home we decided to take some back roads to enjoy the scenery. Much to our surprise, the scenery was nothing but grass, brush, and desolation. There were no houses, just cows and the blazing sun.

My friend looked at her gas gauge. It read "empty." This was kind of surprising, but not too surprising since we had traveled for quite awhile before we noticed it. We kept hoping to find a gas station but had no luck. Now we were becoming concerned.

We did pass an old, dilapidated house. We decided that we would stop and see if someone could give us some help. We knocked on the door. No one answered.

We got back into the old Mercedes. Luckily the engine turned over, even though the gas tank was on "empty." We took off with some anxiety. That is when we started to pray to the Lord to get us safely to a place that had gas. We knew that we wouldn't last long in the hot sun with our little dog, and no water, if we had to walk to a gas station. The road was isolated. Not one car passed us in either direction. We drove miles without seeing any sign of civilization. We were very worried and nervous.

Then, lo and behold, we saw a small trailer park ahead on our right. We thought this would be our only chance to get help. We pulled into the park and knocked on the door that looked like it belonged to the manager of the compound. No one answered. The park looked deserted.

We were really uptight by now. It was very hot outside of the car. Then we spotted two people sitting on a bench outside of a trailer. They were talking to each other.

Next, we approached the man and woman. We told them what had happened to us. The man got up and said he had some gas for our car in a little shed next to his house.

We were so relieved and happy to have them come to our rescue. We told them our prayers were answered. The man came back with a gas container and some crosses in his hand. He said he made nail crosses at his church and wanted us to have some to give to others.

We felt these people had to be angels that were sent by God to help us. We marveled at this for a long time afterward.

seventy

A Beautiful Experience

Give ear to my prayer, O God; and do not
hide Yourself from my supplication.

— Psalms 55:1

AFTER MY EIGHTY-TWO-YEAR-OLD SISTER had been diagnosed with terminal cancer, I brought her to my home. She lived with me in Carpentersville, Illinois, for her remaining days.

As the end was drawing closer, it became increasingly more difficult for her to breathe. She had two days of much labored breathing. One night, at about 10 p.m., I put her to bed. I was very concerned about her, and I couldn't sleep when I went to bed. At about 11:15 p.m., I got up to check on my sister. She was still breathing. I checked her again at 1:30 a.m., and her breathing had worsened, but she was breathing.

I went to the living room to lie on the couch. I started to cry. I begged Jesus to come and take her with Him, to end all of her suffering. **A vision of Jesus appeared to me**. He was dressed in a white tunic with a light blue stole. He had red wavy hair and a red beard. He never talked to me or looked at me. He stood angled toward my sister's bedroom. As He looked in the direction of her room, He held out His hand and then He was gone.

I fell asleep peacefully and woke from a deep sleep about 3:30 a.m. When I went to check on my sister, I found that she had passed away (November 2, 2005). I have never in my life experienced anything like this. It was a beautiful experience.

— *the late Liz La Rocco*

Fifteen Promises of the Blessed Virgin to Christians Who Faithfully Pray the Rosary

1. To all those who shall pray my Rosary devoutly, I promise my special protection and great graces.

2. Those who shall persevere in the recitation of my Rosary will receive some special grace.

3. The Rosary will be a very powerful armor against hell; it will destroy vice, deliver from sin, and dispel heresy.

4. The Rosary will make virtue and good works flourish, and will obtain for souls the most abundant divine mercies. It will draw the hearts of men from the love of the world and its vanities, and will lift them to the desire of eternal things. Oh, that souls would sanctify themselves by this means!

5. Those who trust themselves to me through the Rosary will not perish.

6. Whoever recites my Rosary, devoutly reflecting on the mysteries, shall never be overwhelmed by misfortune. He will not experience the anger of God, nor will he perish by an unprovided death. The sinner will be converted; the just will persevere in grace and merit eternal life.

7. Those truly devoted to my Rosary shall not die without the sacraments of the Church.

8. Those who are faithful to recite my Rosary shall have during their life and at their death the light of God and the plentitude of His graces and will share in the merits of the blessed.

9. I will deliver promptly from purgatory souls devoted to my Rosary.

10. True children of my Rosary will enjoy great glory in heaven.

11. What you shall ask through my Rosary you shall obtain.

12. To those who propagate my Rosary I promise aid in all their necessities.

13. I have obtained from my Son that all the members of the Rosary Confraternity shall have as their intercessors, in life and death, the entire celestial court.

14. Those who recite my Rosary faithfully are my beloved children, the brothers and sisters of Jesus Christ.

15. Devotion to my Rosary is a special sign of predestination.[1]

[1]Rosary Center, Dominican Fathers, Headquarters of the Rosary Confraternity: The Rosary Confraternity's Obligations, Benefits, Indulgences and Promises. Copyright © 2010-1982, Dominican Fathers/The Rosary Center, Portland, Oregon. "Fifteen Promises of the Blessed Virgin to Christians who faithfully pray the Rosary." http://www.rosary-center.org (accessed January 23, 2010).

· ❖ ·

Novena to the Sacred Heart of Jesus

O most holy Heart of Jesus, fountain of every blessing, I adore You, I love You, and with a lively sorrow for my sins, I offer You this poor heart of mine. Make me humble, patient, pure and wholly obedient to Your will. Grant, good Jesus, that I may live in You and for You. Protect me in the midst of danger; comfort me in my afflictions; give me health of body, assistance in my temporal needs, Your blessing on all that I do, and the grace of a holy death.

The Promises of Our Lord to Saint Margaret Mary for Souls Devoted to His Sacred Heart

1. I will give them all the graces necessary in their state of life.
2. I will establish peace in their houses.
3. I will comfort them in all their afflictions.
4. I will be their secure refuge during life, and above all at death.
5. I will bestow a large blessing upon all their undertakings.
6. Sinners shall find in My Heart the source and the infinite ocean of mercy.
7. Tepid souls shall grow fervent.
8. Fervent souls shall quickly mount to high perfection.
9. I will bless every place where a picture of My Heart shall be set up and honored.
10. I will give to priests the gift of touching the most hardened hearts.
11. Those who shall promote this devotion shall have their names written in My Heart, never to be blotted out.
12. I promise in the excessive mercy of My Heart that My all-powerful love will grant to those who communicate on the First Friday in nine consecutive months the grace of final penitence; they shall not die in My disgrace nor without receiving their Sacraments; My Divine Heart shall be their safe refuge in this last moment.

With Ecclesiastical Approbation
Priests of the Sacred Heart
Sacred Heart Monastery
PO Box 900
Hales Corners, Wisconsin 53130-0900
www.poshusa.org

Afterword

I hope you will remember these few thoughts the next time you begin to judge someone. Stop! Realize that we are all God's children. He loves that person as much as He loves you. See the goodness in that person and magnify it. One of my favorite songs by Steven Curtis Chapman is called "Fingerprints of God." In this song are the words, "You are covered with the fingerprints of God." Let us envision the fingerprints of God on all those we meet. —*Heidi R. May*
"Let God inspire you."
Father Eugene J. Faucher